A REOPENING OF CLOSURE

Murray Krieger

A REOPENING OF CLOSURE
Organicism Against Itself

*The Wellek Library Lectures
at the University of California, Irvine*

 COLUMBIA UNIVERSITY PRESS   NEW YORK

Columbia University Press
New York   Oxford
Copyright © 1989 Columbia University Press
All rights reserved

Library of Congress Cataloging-in-Publication Data

Krieger, Murray, 1923–
   A reopening of closure : organicism against itself /
Murray Krieger.
      p.   cm. — (The Weliek Library lectures
at the University of California, Irvine.)
   Bibliography: p.
   Includes index.
   ISBN 0-231-07006-3
   1. Metaphor.   2. Literature, Modern—History and criticism.
3. Criticism.   I. Title.   II. Series.
PN228.M4K75   1989   89-9873
801′.95—dc20   CIP

Casebound editions of Columbia University Press books are Smyth-sewn
and printed on permanent and durable acid-free paper.

⧝   Printed in the United States of America

C 10 9 8 7 6 5 4 3 2 1

To Hazard Adams,
the first Irvine Critic

EDITORIAL NOTE

The Wellek Library Lectures in Critical Theory are given annually at the University of California, Irvine, under the auspices of the Critical Theory Institute. The following lectures were given in May 1988.

The Critical Theory Institute
Mark Poster, Director

CONTENTS

PREFACE

WHEN WE FIRST conceived of the Wellek Library Lectures back in 1980, we hoped that each series of lectures would constitute an extended position paper by a mature scholar reviewing a career and trying to find where it had led, to reexamine the ground on which he or she might momentarily stand—or make a stand—or to find out how slippery it had become. In writing these essays I have tried to respond to that challenge.

In retrospect, instead of being a recapitulation, this undertaking has turned out to be a thoroughly revised version of my earlier work—far more so than I ever anticipated, or, for that matter, intended. In rereading the three chapters I find that each is, in effect, a rewriting, from my current perspective, of an earlier book that I believe marked an important stage in my thinking. The first chapter seems to have turned out to be a rewriting of *A Window to Criticism: Shakespeare's* Sonnets *and Modern Poetics* (1964), the second a rewriting of *The New Apologists for Poetry* (1956), and the third a rewriting of *The Tragic Vision: Variations on a Theme in Literary Interpretation* (1960).

What I find more remarkable is my sense that these three works seem now to have been parts of a single project—or at least their rewritings, if only in the form they take here, seem so to me. The effects on my theorizing and my criticism of the many recent developments in theory, together with my stubbornness in hanging onto certain notions in the face of these developments, are all well reflected in these essays, which do—as I hoped they would—pretty well indicate where I am in relation to where I have come from. The place, I now think, is pretty well and consistently defined in the chapters that follow. But I hope that I do not stop examining its grounds in response to the shifting of the ground around it, for it is only by that sort of activity that I have managed, after these decades, to have come there.

I hope that, in addressing the many challenges of recent theorists, I have honestly found ways to accommodate within my thinking what I found useful in them and have not merely given ground before them in order to keep my writing abreast of what is current and fashionable. I hope, in other words, that my adjustments have occurred for sound theoretical reasons and not for makeshift reasons suited to the changing politics of theory. Of course, I want to believe that my work has been enriched and deepened, that it has grown in theoretical power, as a result of the developments wrought through my reading and debating, but I must confess occasional anxiety that I would hardly know if the motives behind my responses to recent challenges were more suspect. So I hope the reader will find cause to welcome the more charitable interpretation, as I try to persuade myself of it.

In writing these chapters I had in mind three principal objectives that I meant them to serve. I wanted to conceive anew the relation of the semiotic of literary metaphor to the semiotic of the metaphors of faith, and the relation of them both to the development of organicism. Further, I wanted to rewrite the story of organicism as both a nineteenth-century and a modernist doctrine in order to correct some of the simplified versions produced for the convenience of those anxious to refute it. In other words, I wanted to trace and authorize a tradition of interpretation that has not yet lost its power with us if we treat it with the subtlety I claim to find in it. Finally, I wanted to reexamine the relation of literature to political history, to ask whether the literary text can play beyond where history dictates.

It may be useful for me briefly to outline the sequence of my chapters:

The first deals with the sources—or at least the precursors—that I find for the organicist theory of metaphor in the typological workings of Renaissance poems. But I want to show how double-edged these workings are and how much they contribute to complications in later theories of organicism.

The second deals with the adaptation of such typological workings into nineteenth- and twentieth-century theories of organicism, an adaptation that encourages, within those theories, a counter-movement that anticipates the explicit anti-organicism that has propelled theorists during the last several decades.

The concluding chapter seeks to extend the coexistence of the positive and negative thrusts in the organicist theory of metaphor— by now seen as facing both ways—by using it to probe the limits and the ambiguous contours of fictional and existential identity within literary texts.

Most of these pages were written in Konstanz, Federal Republic of Germany, during periods in 1986 and 1987 while I held the *Forschungspreis* of the Alexander von Humboldt-*Stiftung*. I am grateful to the German government and to the Humboldt-*Stiftung* for this rare honor and, consequently, for their generous support.

It has been a great privilege for me to have been invited by my Irvine colleagues to join my distinguished predecessors in this series. I must thank them, not only for this invitation, but, more importantly, for their intellectual comradeship over the years, first in our Focused Research Program in Contemporary Critical Theory and now in the newly established Critical Theory Institute. It was in the broadening forced upon me by our many discussions that the re-thinkings which led to these rewritings were instigated and nourished. Finally, I must thank Joan Krieger who, both verbally and graphically, has been my one non-institutional critic—of theory and of my theory, of prose and of my prose—all along.

Murray Krieger
Laguna Beach, California
February 1989

A REOPENING OF CLOSURE

CHAPTER ONE

THE FIGURE IN THE RENAISSANCE POEM AS BOUND AND UNBOUNDED

The profane secularizes the Sacred Realm to the point where the latter is the only secular thing left.

Theodor Adorno,
"On the Relation between Art and Society,"
Aesthetic Theory

THESE ESSAYS ARE NOT intended as a last-ditch attempt to defend a now-outmoded aesthetic, though undoubtedly there are those who will choose to view them as such. Nor are they an attempt to resurrect the New Criticism (surely by now a futile attempt in any case), though many of their prejudices can, I fear, be traced to vestiges of that movement. Finally, I do not want to offer once more to theory the metaphor of organicism as if we can take it seriously as an analogy for the work of art. But I do mean to suggest that the aesthetic and philosophical tradition we associate with organicism has had lurking within it tendencies that would break open the closed structures we have usually attributed to it, especially when we wish to bring it under attack by our postmodern resistances to any such closure. I want to look into those tendencies in hopes of finding in them their own resistance, a resistance that anticipates the revolution of postmodern theory and so makes that theory less revolutionary. In other words, I intend to offer a version that is also a *sub*version of organicism.

I

So I want to reopen closure in two senses, one theoretical and one substantive. I want to reopen the very question of whether the issue of textual closure in poetry is a closed one (and the assumption for some time has been that it is); but I can reopen this question only by asking us to reexamine the interpretive tradition associated with textual closure in order to find suggestions in it of opening what it appears to have sealed.

As most of us deal with the aesthetic tradition that we think of as running from (at least) Immanuel Kant to the modernism we associate with the New Criticism, we tend to close the question of closure by insisting that this tradition (a closed tradition) has developed a monolithic system dependent upon closure both within the aesthetic object and within our aesthetic experience of that object, that experience being controlled—and thus closed—by the force of closure in the object. Thus in the very act of reopening closure as a theoretical issue again to be discussed, we are reopening the substantive claim of textual closure, a claim too often associated unquestioningly with the critical tradition after Kant.

Let me at the outset acknowledge that previous commentators have indeed called attention to those subtler organicists who have pressed their theory to provide for a countermovement to closure— for a "variety" to balance the call for "unity." But there are few systematic attempts to describe the movement of organicism beyond closure, to find in its self-embrace an opening that would expose its apparently monolithic claims to a self-generating opposition. Such is my attempt here.

One cannot exaggerate the place of Kant in the development of this tradition as it has been reconstructed by those who would destroy its lingering influence. Far more than his own text would justify, Kant is seen as responsible for the claim that the aesthetic experience—and before that the work—depends upon a sense of "internal purposiveness" that must lead us to see its form as a closed form. Indeed, our very way of perceiving—from Kant to the Gestaltists to E. H. Gombrich—has seemed to depend on a pressure toward finding or making a unifying form as a psychologically perceptual form. However, from as far back as Aristotle we inherited the reading habit, vitally reinforced since the late eighteenth century, of looking for a principle of structure that would serve a totalizing functionalism. We have habitually been assuming, in other words, that there ought to be some rationalization to justify why any particular element of a text is included in the text and why it is placed where it is rather than somewhere else. ("As therefore, in the other imitative arts, the imitation is one when the object imitated is one, so the plot, being an imitation of an action, must imitate one action, and that a whole, the structural union of the parts being such that, if any one of them is displaced or removed, the whole will be disjointed and disturbed. For a thing whose presence or absence makes no visible difference is not an organic part of whole" [chapter 8 of *The Poetics* in the Butcher translation].)

Even today, in the midst of flourishing theories that would celebrate all that resists such unifying claims—theories that would celebrate margins rather than centers, the aporia rather than the filled gap, the arbitrary or even the random rather than the necessary—even today, most of our essays that seek to interpret texts usually do so by trying to account for why any particular textual element became the way it is and why it found its way into the text where it did. To ask "why" in these matters is to acknowledge that there ought to be a reason, and—whatever the source of the rationalization—we would expect such a reason to be derived from some overall hypothesis about a form, a closed form, even if that form is one we prefer to think of as historical or cultural. So, however narrow or broad our conception of the text at hand—from the words on the page to the social-historical discursive formation to the seamless web of textuality itself—we seem to have an "aesthetic" need to confer authority upon it in order to help us make sense of its elements. And we seem unable to shake this reading habit, perhaps because it derives from a perceptual habit.

All this is only to remind us that, in the tradition we associate with Kant and his forebears (Baumgarten, Mendelssohn, etc.), the "aesthetic" begins in sense perception, and sense perception is a matter of closure, of seeking out of raw sense-data to construct objects, whole objects upon which we can act in actual experience.

And, from Kant to Benedetto Croce, theorists see a continuum, dependent on the model of sense perception, running from the merest act of visually grasping an everyday object to the most elegant response to a beautiful painting. (This continuum is perhaps most explicitly set forth in the monistic idealism of Croce, whose single term, "intuition," must serve every step—which is to say, every kind of activity—along the way.) And perceptual psychologists remind us that it may well be our interpretive need to fill in (in effect, to complete) our visual field that led these theorists to posit aesthetic closure for art objects and our responses to them.[1]

Yet, if we now speak of the aesthetic response to a single text, any suggestion of totality—of a single principle unique to this text but universally governing its particulars within the text—is seen as unduly, and dangerously, exclusionary. Analogizing (as many have come to do) the text to a body politic, one could see a unifying principle as not only totalizing but also totalitarian, so that the text as a closed system becomes a closed society and hence repressive. As a consequence of its idolatrous development from Idealism to Romanticism to Modernism, closure itself—closure in a myriad of guises—comes to be seen as the disease in need of postmodernist therapy. The attack on closure that has in recent years become so politically sensitive slides easily—perhaps at times too easily—from the metaphysical-political realm (closed systems such as those ultimately realized in Hegelianism) to the linguistic (the verbal enforcement produced by the hegemonic discourse within a Foucaultian episteme) to the aesthetic (the exclusionary power of the self-fulfilling text, now condemned by the wariness of totalization and kept in control by the political consciousness—conscious as it must try to be of the "political unconscious," whether of authors or of theorist-critics).

It is a large question whether it is adequate as argument, or even at all sensible, to apply the political analogy universally, and particularly to texts, seeing them as simulacra of their societies, without subjecting the analogy to criticism; but I postpone dealing with it for now. Still, however we answer this question, we should recognize the structural similarity between arguments for and arguments against closure. The attack on closure derives from the application of the political analogy—derives, that is, from abhorrence of a totalized system and fear of its repressive consequences—and, in traditional theory moving *toward* closure, as we have seen, the aesthetics of unity derives from its analogizing of aesthetic perception to the perception of the whole objects we act upon in everyday life. For the latter, the perception of wholeness is seen to move outward and upward to the perception of aesthetic wholes, wholes that—in their closure—sponsor a wholeness in the psychological experience of responding to them, moving from that to a wholeness in the person as a psychic unit and even to his or her culture as an anthropological unit, in a historical moment now seen also with its own defined integrity. So the outwardly enlarging—and yet enclosing—circle either moves constructively, via the very metaphor of the circle as enclosure, from everyday perception to aesthetics via sensory psychology, or moves menacingly from metaphysics to aesthetics via politics, depending on whether one argues on behalf of closure or wants to condemn it.

The tendency to seek closure—beginning as perceptual and for the modernist mind sustained as metaphysical—can be seen as deriving from the organicist model, first in philosophy, then in aesthetics, and then in literary theory. We must remember (and for the last decades we have often enough been reminded) that organicism begins and ends as metaphor. It lives and thrives because it takes itself as metaphor seriously—which is to say literally—and it is deprived of its power by those who look into its metaphor and unground it, often because of their own political motives that turn into their own metaphors. The biological ground of the organic metaphor, so often discredited, interests me less—as we shall see—than its theological ground.

Yet one must concede the biological analogy out of which the metaphor moves: I will treat as the center of organicism its claim that the regulative principle of growth in the created entity must be internally derived and internally directed. This means that all that is external to the organism can be taken into it only to be absorbed, reshaped, and indeed reconstituted within its internally defined needs.

As the empowering motive of organicism, this claim is the formalistic center of Aristotle's *Poetics* (especially chapters 7–10), in which he justifies the integrity of the constructed poem, in contrast to empirical reality (Aristotle's "history" as the chronicle of "what is"), by appealing to the poem's self-reinforcing wholeness. But of course it is in what nineteenth- and twentieth-century theorists drew out of Kant's "internal purposiveness," as a second coming of that Aristotelian notion, that the doctrine of organicism was made usable for modernist critics. Echoing Coleridge's elevation of "imagination" over "fancy," it supported the prizing of "symbol" at the expense of "allegory" as the elevation of the internally self-sufficient over the dependence on external entities that maintain their meanings intact.[2]

This semiotic preference of symbol to allegory carries with it a definition of metaphor as the one figure that captures all originally external things within itself and, having transformed them, identifies them with (and within) itself. Of course, this is to speak of metaphor in the most radical sense (in contrast to simile or analogy or, more currently, metonymy). It requires, in its quest for verbal presence, a total identity of the two elements collapsed into the figure instead of settling for mere similarity, which permits difference as well as similarity to remain as characteristics of the two elements, still grasped as two, with some remainder—large or small—incommensurate and so unabsorbed.

It is no accident that Coleridge formulates his most explicit statement of the distinction between symbol and allegory in a theological context in which the one text that concerns him is the Bible.[3] He has accurately judged the extent to which the language authorized by religious mystery serves, in our tradition, as the model for poetic metaphor; the extent to which our response to the transubstantiating act of metaphor has been molded by the claims of a faith that created its language habits as ours. Hence the terms of poetic closure —as the very semiotic ground for the organic aesthetic—arise out of the presences asserted by Christianity, out of the sacramental vision that literalizes metaphor in the language of Christian ritual. Through the mysteries of Christ's double—and doubly paradoxical —status as man and as God, the worldly body can contain the undying spirit, as worldly history can contain the eschatological or the Old Testament can contain the New. And the verbal sign in poetry, dedicated to metaphor-as-symbol on the Christian semiotic model, can function with a similar effect of an incarnating presence, as signs in nonpoetic discourse cannot. As Christ is literalized in the world and the eternal Christian pattern is actualized in the finitude and temporal sequence of human history, so the metaphor becomes literalized in the poem—and, for the critic, the metaphor of the poem as organism itself becomes literalized in organic theory, which uncritically accepts the mystification. On the religious analogy, the organic critic is thus licensed to identify the poetic text with a living body, treating its word as substance, indeed as flesh.

It is out of assumptions such as these that the *figura,* as a specially privileged—if paradoxical—sign, worked for literary historians like Erich Auerbach, who made this typological pattern available for literary interpretation to critics like me. As a form of semiotic magic, the *figura* claimed to be authorized by the mutual reinforcement between linguistic realms whose terms appear to be mutually exclusive, indeed contradictory. The typological habit urges the reader to see every textual event doubly (at least),[4] both as an unrepeatable chunk of worldly history caught in the stream of time and as an element in a fixed pattern that, though transcendent, is immanently —and thus always—present in history. As with the several figures of the Old Testament fulfilled in the one Christ story of the New, the historical figure, existentially trapped in the unredeemable birth-to-death sequence of the single life, is metaphorically "figured" as part of an ever-redeeming design whose fulfillment is both later and —in the typological scheme—already now. The figure is only a historical cipher and yet is also *in* the fulfillment that converts mere figure into typological *figura.*

But this complex sense of the figural had to be extended beyond Dante, for whom in Auerbach it could be seen as functioning in a literal sense for a poet of Christian orthodoxy, so that it could be taken as a way to read all poetic texts in our tradition—secular as well as devout—that came to be seen as invoking a typological hermeneutic. This hermeneutic is now "revealed" (no longer by holy scripture, but) by the critic whose terms, because derived from the aesthetics of organicism, can open up these texts through the critic's unique power to replicate the power of their special language. This interpretive practice explains my treatment of Shakespeare's *Sonnets* in *A Window to Criticism* (1964), with typology functioning as my window to *them*.

Here, however, what I want to insist upon is the difference between the use of this language of presence, of literalized metaphor, in theology (or in poetry leaning upon theological orthodoxy) and its use in secular poetry—in the Petrarchan sonnets, for example, as distinguished from the *Commedia* of Dante. I believe that, to some extent, the partly inaccurate grounds for the dismissal of the organic tradition in recent years can be traced to the failure to distinguish between the theological semiotic and the secular borrowing of certain elements from the theological semiotic. The charge of the sacralization of poetry made against organicism assumes too simply that such borrowing must be uncritical and blind, though it is a borrowing with a difference (or with an awareness of difference), a borrowing that often is conscious of—and even exploits— the consequences of a semiotic built out of the loss of theological substance.

The total collapse of semiotic distance in the miraculous transformation that permits an identity of presences may occur in the metaphor that governs the Christian mystery, but that distance is in part —even if grudgingly—restored to consciousness once the same principle of metaphor is taken out of the literally Christian sign-system and is applied to an analogous profane structure that the poet uses as if it was the religious one, one calling for an identical treatment and seeking to earn a similar magical effect. The presence of God in the historical creature of Christ, like that of His body and His blood in bread and wine, can work linguistically only if it springs from a literal belief in the divine-human paradox. It becomes the model for the operation of metaphor in the language of our poetry as a secular art, perhaps because we have sought to sacralize that art, securing for it the benefits of a theologically grounded metaphor by imposing the model of that metaphor upon it. But the

opposite cause may be as reasonable: that the imposition of the
metaphorical structure upon unworthy materials—perhaps materials arousing skepticism rather than inspiring faith—is a de-sacralizing of metaphor and not a sacralizing of art.

This returns us to my insistence on the difference between the
literal force of the metaphor in its original theological form and the
uncertainties and self-consciousness that attend it in its profane
adaptations, however careful the poet may be about the apparent
authenticity of the borrowed structure he imposes. And this difference is, I repeat, that even in the apparent assertion of identity
between its elements—of a presence of one *in* the other—some
semiotic distance has been inserted when the metaphor is borrowed
for profane uses. How, then, can we still see it as metaphor? Metaphor, as I have defined it within its theological origins, depends
upon the conviction of identity—the elimination of all semiotic
distance between two entities, so that they exchange properties and
are confounded as one thing, as entities lost in the *id* of *identity*.
How, then, in the profane adaptation, can the perceived awareness
of the borrowings of metaphoric form and its imposition on non-
sacred materials in order to bestow a magic upon them—how can
this awareness help but sponsor a skepticism that would preclude
the metaphoric effect and move us from metaphor to metonym or,
as Paul de Man puts it, from symbol to allegory?

I want to argue for a criticism that, confronted by such profane
poems, responds at once to the sense of metaphoric identity *and* to
the awareness of semiotic distance that should preclude metaphor.
Yet in these cases the two responses, instead of creating a mutual
blockage, reinforce one another. In accord with such a criticism, we
would feel the power of metaphor even while, with the poem's
encouragement, we would feel the inappropriateness of the application.

In the case of a Petrarchan sonnet, for example, we can respond
both to the words of the poet-lover who is the persona and to the
voice beyond which controls the poem and yet, by undermining the
completeness of the persona's vision, controls it only by allowing it
to break apart. Introducing undecidability, that voice controls it as

not only undecidable, but as decidedly undecidable. From inside the persona, within the vision of his words, we read the expression of a profane lover's faith that supervises a transubstantiating act that seems to earn itself, or better yet to create itself, in the language of metaphor; and yet, from outside him, the voice beyond acknowledges that closed affirmation as an exaggeration of misplaced claims that has uncritically submitted to mystification. We may perceive the poem to be sacralizing the profane, and so raising it to a human divinity earned by the metaphorical transfer of properties, but only as it profanes the sacred by reminding us that it is all a sacrilege performed by a secular supplicant who would remake and elevate his act of love. As sacrilege it calls the sacred into doubt by forcing it into the *un*magical dimensions of the human while retaining its very own terms. But the human realm is raised in the process, though only to the extent that we permit the metaphor to function. If it can be raised only as we credit the metaphor, we can, despite the skepticism we bring to bear, still respond with sympathetic wonder to the human impulse that would sacralize the precious in our experience by insisting on making it eligible for metaphor.

Yet the metaphor, in the subliminal incongruities between its form and its matter—that is, between the substantive demands of its inherited form and the indecorous substance to which that form is applied—functions in part as what might be termed a mock-metaphor; for it reveals a winking awareness that the identity that the speaker's claim to metaphor must have as nothing less than complete is at the same time radically incomplete. In its way it functions much as we have more commonly observed the mock-heroic to function, at once getting all the dignity—all the uplift—it can through a rhetoric that would earn for its lowly though self-important subject its elevated treatment and yet pointing up the absurd grandiosity of such a subject claiming that right to such false eloquence.

My several treatments of Pope's "The Rape of the Lock"—themselves bordering on the idolatrous—insisted precisely on this double power: the power of metaphor totally sustained and yet the power of mock-metaphor totally subversive of the other power, revealing all as mere metonymy. It is the power of an idolatry (of the lock of hair) that we are persuaded to find empty though the poem's language appears to make it full, and deservedly full. This is the double power that in *The Classic Vision* (1971) I called "systematic duplicity," the systematic duplicity of "metonymic metaphor."[5]

In this view the mock-heroic may be seen as a model for all varieties of mock-metaphor in that it is a more blatant and self-conscious version of it, straining almost to the breaking point the incongruities between metaphoric form and an inappropriate subject on which it is imposed. Of course the mock-heroic, functioning in the post-Renaissance air of the late seventeenth and eighteenth centuries, can make the break between subject and metaphorical apparatus more evident, more self-aware, even sheerly outrageous, as the Renaissance—or, even more, the Middle Ages—could not, since their sense of the sacred, in its collision with the profane, was blurred by a language that was far less openly parodic.

This contrast between neoclassical mock-heroic and Renaissance mock-metaphor is instructive. In the mock-heroic the split announces a duality, with a division that few besides Pope could manage to overcome by turning duality into a verbal duplicity from which oneness is not altogether precluded. In the mock-metaphor (which is also the metaphor) that I see in the Renaissance, the duplicity works in an opposite and subtler way: the appropriation of the sacred metaphor and its metaphoric workings is made to seem so "natural" that we accept the unity as secure; and duality comes later, almost as an afterthought (*our* afterthought), as the union is undermined and turned against itself by a nagging skepticism that reveals the language habit of metaphor as "conventional" only, though it is this convention that is the enabling act of this poetry, and perhaps—for the Renaissance poet—of profane love itself.[6]

There are several different sacralizing moves made by Renaissance metaphors in poems that would open to our skepticism all that their mystifications seek to have closed. We might, for one, consider the metaphorical habit in Renaissance love poetry—indeed since the poetry of Medieval Troubadors—that scholars have long classified

as Mariolatry. It leads the poet to see in his beloved—even during
moments of physical attraction—the sacred attributes of the Virgin
Mary, somehow confounding earthly love with heavenly love because his lady seems to inspire him to both. Her human-divine
attributes can lead him to pursue his love as earthly, or to purify it
because—alas—it is earthly, or—paradoxically—to do both at once.
We can see these several possibilities, either distinguished from one
another or overlapping, in endless numbers of Petrarchan sonnets,
indeed in the very narrative model behind the Petrarchan sonnet.
These possibilities are juggled unevenly, and not always well, but
for us instructively, in Spenser's *Amoretti*. These poems often affirm
the beloved as a sacred object, in effect a Virgin Mary, though they
barely and only occasionally betray a sense of the impropriety, even
the sacrilege, of doing so as her would-be earthly lover. This is to
say that they implicitly acknowledge that she is functioning as anything but Mary since the love she inspires in the speaker—however
he may mystify it with his primal metaphor—is anything but sacred,
so that the speaker's metaphor is in the process turned into a mock-
metaphor.

The conflict between desire and chastity leads the poet to use
classical poetic machinery while invoking the Christian to deny it its
sensual consequences. Thus the octave of Sonnet 8:

> More than most fair, full of the living fire,
> Kindled above unto the maker near:
> No eyes but joys, in which all powers conspire,
> That to the world naught else be counted dear.
> Through your bright beams doth not the blinded guest
> Shoot out his darts to base affections wound:
> But angels come to lead frail minds to rest
> In chaste desires on heavenly beauty bound.
>   (Spellings modernized)

The metaphorical impetus would make his love one with heaven,
thus leading even Cupid's darts and their targets ("base affections")
to the higher objectives dictated by angels for "frail minds": to the
heavenly land of "chaste desires." But the oxymoron "chaste desires"

quivers in its internal contradiction, perhaps reminding us that the all-too-human mind remains "frail," still weakened by "base affections."

Spenser is sometimes too soberly and singlemindedly Platonic to mock his metaphor by questioning how human desire can be at once chaste and aflame, how it can be chaste while still being desire; or how its object can both inspire desire and make it oppose itself. His beloved's saintliness seems unchallenged in Sonnet 22:

> This holy season fit to fast and pray,
> Men to devotion ought to be inclined:
> Therefore I likewise on so holy day
> For my sweet Saint some service fit will find.
> Her temple fair is built within my mind,
> In which her glorious image placèd is,
> On which my thoughts do day and night attend
> Like sacred priests that never think amiss.
> There I to her as th'author of my bliss
> Will build an altar to appease her ire:
> And on the same my heart will sacrifice,
> Burning in flames of pure and chaste desire:
>   The which vouchsafe O goddess to accept
>   Amongst thy dearest relics to be kept.

The poet yields to his metaphor without resistance, unconcerned about the friction between chastity and desire, between flames as purifying and flames as sensual heat, unconcerned about the difference between his lady and the saint in the kind of responses aroused in him. He is, in other words, insufficiently alert to the mistake in his metaphorical equation. His speaker's sensual deprivation at the hands of his lady may become half-voluntary in a quasi-theological rationalization. Although her constant denial forces him to suffer the unalleviated protraction of his agonizing and the incurable state of a desire never satisfied, he welcomes that denial in imitation of the model of an ascetic religion, although he seems unaware that he has retreated from the two-sidedness of his metaphor.

Even when Spenser's speaker celebrates the surrender of his be-

loved to his importunings (Sonnets 63–85), he presses the identity
of the sensual and spiritual, unaware of their opposed characteristics
that, as he presents them, would also render them mutually exclusive. At times he falls victim to an utter confusion in which the
pleasures of sense, having become the lover's false metaphor for
heaven, are mistaken for the sacred, sense-free, Platonic and Christian
heaven. His discourse seems explicit in acknowledging the difference—in recognizing the mock-metaphor as well as affirming the
metaphor—except that he concludes as if the total identity of a metaphor unsubverted would hold. Sonnet 72 is an excellent example.

> Oft when my spirit doth spread her bolder wings,
> In mind to mount up to the purest sky:
> It down is weighed with thought of earthly things
> And clogged with burden of mortality,
> Where when that sovereign beauty it doth spy,
> Resembling heaven's glory in her light:
> Drawn with sweet pleasure's bait, it back doth fly,
> And unto heaven forgets her former flight.
> There my frail fancy fed with full delight,
> Doth bathe in bliss and mantleth most at ease:
> Nor thinks of other heaven, but how it might
> Her heart's desire with most contentment please.
>   Heart need not with none other happiness,
>   But here on earth to have such heaven's bliss.

In the speaker's anxiety to make his beloved both of heaven and of
earth, on both sides he doubles the exaggerations of metaphor and
piety in the confusion between Platonic and sensual values. The
speaker early concedes that his beloved only resembles "heaven's
glory" but is not heaven itself, is indeed its opposite, since, of earth,
she—because of her misleading resemblance to heaven—draws him
back to earth from his intended flight to heaven, where he could be
freed of his "burden of mortality" (composed, presumably, of his
sensual attraction to her). Misled by this earthly substitute, his "frail
fancy" is amply stuffed. Apparently the "burden of mortality" has
only been increased, so that the "purest sky" of that "other heaven"

(that is, the real—or rather the ideal—one) is utterly dismissed by the anti-Platonic lover. Yet the sonnet concludes with his use of the term "heaven" as appropriate to her: his confident equation of the two heavens in her, as heaven enough for him and with no awareness of the mortal error in judgment into which he has been seduced. The heaven-on-earth of the final line, an empty hyperbole, has little in common with the "other heaven" ("purest sky") so that it would seem to have little claim to the word "heaven" which earlier in the poem is restrictively defined by its exclusion of the earthly. But the poet prefers to overlook the difference between a superficial resemblance to heaven—coexisting with crucial oppositions—and the equivalence proclaimed by unqualified metaphor. Oblivious to his limitations as a poet of profane love, Spenser often remains too one-sided in his Platonism to take poetic advantage of the double edge of the secularized Christian metaphor, and so cannot break open its enclosure.

Because Spenser fails to recognize the mock-metaphor already present in the secular adaptation of Christian metaphor, he is less adept a manipulator of the Mariolatrous conceits of courtly love than is a shrewdly self-conscious Petrarchan sonneteer like Sir Philip Sidney. Though Sidney's allusions are more classical than Christian, he follows a similar metaphorical quest; but his counter-metaphorical thrust is much keener. His poet-lover treats his Stella both as a literal star and as merely a name, a proper noun that leads the parade of empty words. In this second, mock-metaphorical perspective, Stella is no more than a projected sign that represents his desire to see her as a star, a desire that is realized as for him in his mystified rapture she becomes this star.

Sonnet 28, for example, is an allegory that denies itself by insisting that Stella is not an allegory—an empty, bookish sign for star —but the actual transcendent thing itself.

> You that with allegory's curious frame,
> Of others' children changelings use to make,
> With me those pains for God's sake do not take:
> I list not dig so deep for brazen fame.

> When I say "Stella," I do mean the same
> Princess of Beauty, for whose only sake
> The reins of Love I love, though never slake,
> And joy therein, though nations count it shame.
> I beg no subject to use eloquence,
> Nor in hid ways do guide Philosophy:
> Look at my hands for no such quintessence;
> But know that I in pure simplicity
>   Breathe out the flames which burn within my heart,
>   Love only reading unto me this art.

Rejecting those learned poets who with "eloquence" and "Philosophy" use "allegory's curious frame" to make "Of others' children changelings," this poet, guided only by love, would turn from learning to "pure simplicity." Yet all that he writes carries its own allegorical extravagance even while he proclaims it as the simple literal truth:

> When I say "Stella," I do mean the same
> Princess of Beauty, for whose only sake
> The reins of love I love, though never slake,
> And joy therein, though nations count it shame.

Such claims are to constitute no more than an artless and unadorned text of the heart, even as he inflates it:

> But know that I in pure simplicity
> Breathe out the flames which burn within my heart,
> Love only reading unto me this art.

Presumably this is direct and full verbal representation rather than the empty exaggerations of allegory, though its every word, its every outrageously extravagant word, calls itself into doubt.

Or there are several sonnets in which the invocation of the very name "Stella" produces a magic nominalism, as into the name the sacred person is incarnated, transforming reality, even making it act in ways contrary to itself, as in the paradox of Christian miracle. In Sonnet 35 ("What may words say, or what may words not say") all

words—with the sole exception of the name "Stella"—are made by
her present reality to belie the nature of their referents, thereby
proving their emptiness ("Where truth itself must speak like flattery," "Where Nature doth with infinite agree," and, in the spirit of
Petrarchism, as in Spenser, "Where Cupid is sworn page to Chastity"). But her name, thanks to her being, is a self-fulfilling word:
". . . long needy Fame / Doth even grow rich, naming my Stella's
name." (And of course Stella's name—her married name, ironically
—happens to be Rich.) Or in Sonnet 106 ("Oh absent presence,
Stella is not here") the poet uses the name as a magical invocation
to presence: "Stella, I say my Stella, should appear." (Of course,
now, almost at the end of the sequence, we see in this sonnet that
the magic has begun to fail: she remains absent.)

Or there is, in Sonnet 74, Sidney's half-idolatrous, half-comic
treatment of Stella as his muse, literalizing the classical metaphor of
divine and transformative inspiration in her most earthly kiss be-
stowed upon the prosaic speaker, raising him into a poet and his
discourse into poetry.

> I never drank of Aganippe well,
> Nor ever did in shade of Tempe sit:
> And Muses scorn with vulgar brains to dwell,
> Poor Layman I, for sacred rites unfit.
> Some do I hear of Poets' fury tell,
> But (God wot) wot not what they mean by it:
> And this I swear by blackest brook of hell,
> I am no pick-purse of another's wit.
> How falls it then, that with so smooth an ease
> My thoughts I speak, and what I speak doth flow
> In verse, and that my verse best wits doth please?
> Guess we the cause: "What, is it thus?" Fie no:
>   "Or so?" Much less: "How then?" Sure thus it is:
>   My lips are sweet, inspired with Stella's kiss.

He has, through identifying her with her classical counterpart, fully
empowered her as his muse. Yet he arouses our half-amused awareness of the trivial reality of the kiss and the absurd exaggeration of

its effects as the muse's instrument of inspiration, so that we feel the mock-metaphorical accompaniment to the total metaphor that the poem appears to proclaim. For we feel, and are meant to feel, the extent to which the metaphor is a mistake, even a silly mistake.[7]

Of course, we have already seen that this countermovement that strips and exposes metaphor—what I am calling mock-metaphor— is as likely to be serious as humorous. In his *Sonnets* Shakespeare often follows the same model of total metaphorical union that we have observed in Spenser and Sidney, and with most serious effects. Among his several claims of union, I want to concentrate here on the magical transfer that applies the typological model, with the beloved functioning as the fulfillment of earlier figures. Different individuals in history, or in the poet's personal history, who have lived and died their separate existences, are represented—that is, achieve a new present, a new presence—in the single consummate identity of the poet's beloved. Or at least the speaker, in his enraptured state, is persuaded of the completeness of this metaphorical transfer.

For example, Sonnets 30 and 31 (beginning "When to the sessions of sweet silent thought") trace the endless mourning endured by the poet for the loss of his past friends to death, a payment of his sorrow that is never to be completed, never paid in full. It is a sorrow beyond the accountability of such banking-house terms. Yet the mere thought of his present living friend miraculously brings compensation (by the end of Sonnet 30: "All losses are restor'd and sorrows end"), a compensation irrationally rationalized when, in Sonnet 31, that friend is described as incorporating all past friends, thereby claiming their love as his own:

> Thy bosom is endearèd with all hearts
> Which I by lacking have supposèd dead;
> And there reigns love and all love's loving parts,
> And all those friends which I thought burièd.
> How many a holy and obsequious tear
> Hath dear religious love stol'n from mine eye,
> As interest of the dead, which now appear

> But things remov'd that hidden in thee lie!
> Thou art the grave where buried love doth live,
> Hung with the trophies of my lovers gone,
> Who all their parts of me to thee did give:
> That due of many now is thine alone.
>   Their images I lov'd I view in thee,
>   And thou—all they—hast all the all of me.

For the speaker, present reality absorbs and *real*izes the multiple images of a now absent past, the "all" overriding the distinctions carried by each individual in one pool of a single identity. And yet the language of accounting, insisted upon throughout Sonnet 30, asserts itself still in 31 to undermine the extravagant mystifications that would override the realm of arithmetic distinctions.

Or in Sonnet 106 the sequence of individuals in the written history of our culture ("the chronicle of wasted time") similarly culminates and dissolves in the present beloved.

> When in the chronicle of wasted time
> I see descriptions of the fairest wights,
> And beauty making beautiful old rhyme
> In praise of ladies dead and lovely knights,
> Then, in the blazon of sweet beauty's best,
> Of hand, of foot, of lip, of eye, of brow,
> I see their antique pen would have express'd
> Even such a beauty as you master now.
> So all their praises are but prophecies
> Of this our time, all you prefiguring;
> And, for they look'd but with divining eyes,
> They had not skill enough your worth to sing:
>   For we, which now behold these present days,
>   Have eyes to wonder, but lack tongues to praise.

In this sonnet the speaker seems convinced of the literal workings of typology, with his beloved as a final presence, the ultimate fulfillment of all previous "figures," the one Coming as a New Testament that acts eschatologically upon all history ("So all their praises [of

older figures] are but prophecies / Of this our time, all you prefiguring.") The very alliteration, as an echo in which this final reappear-
ance resounds, argues for itself as transformative ("praises" into
"prophecies" into the "prefiguring" that works its typological magic
in producing the present consummation). It is as if the identity of
sound in the signifiers were enough to create the single identity of a
fully realized signified. Yet the sonnet firmly denies the efficacy of
language, its capacity to represent the friend's present perfection. It
is a failure both of the prefiguring language of the past ("for they
look'd but with divining eyes, / They had not skill enough your
worth to sing") and the would-be descriptive language of the present ("For we, which now behold these present days, / Have eyes to
wonder, but lack tongues to praise"). This ultimate paragon stands
at the end of time, beyond all earlier language, which lacked reference, and—though we can look—beyond ours too. The poem
points to—and celebrates—what it confesses itself unable to represent. It outdoes all language and yet finally fails itself. Again the
poet is locked in the paradox of language as both magical and
deficient.

In many of the sonnets the speaker finds the entire world about
him transfigured in the presence of his beloved. Sonnets 113–14
are exemplary. The speaker's eye, controlled by his mind, "no form
delivers to the heart / Of bird, of flow'r, or shape which it doth
latch," except through the beauty and perfection of the beloved.

> For if it see the rud'st or gentlest sight,
> The most sweet favour or deformèd'st creature,
> The mountain or the sea, the day or night,
> The crow or dove, it shapes them to your feature.

But here as elsewhere in the *Sonnets,* the speaker draws back from
any claim that the world is actually transformed ("My most true
mind thus mak'th mine eye untrue"). Instead he retreats to the realm
of his own private psychology, to his own perceptual illusions sponsored by love.

Or whether doth my mind, being crowned with you,
Drink up the monarch's plague, this flattery,
Or whether shall I say mine eye saith true,
And that your love taught it this alchemy . . . ?
O, 'tis the first!—'tis flattery in my seeing.

The magic that would alchemize the world dissolves into the self-hypnosis that only flatters it: the fallen world is not raised; it is only seen through love's psychology as better than it deserves to be: "To make of monsters and things indigest / Such cherubins as your sweet self resemble, / Creating every bad a perfect best . . . 'tis flattery in my seeing." Yet the vision is not for that given up but is rather embraced the more dearly as the joyous reward of a love-filled private consciousness. ("If it be poison'd, 'tis the lesser sin / That mine eye loves it and doth first begin.")

Both the metaphor and the collapse of the metaphor are sustained in these poems, which themselves drift into open-ended divagations each moment they affirm their sealed completeness. Similarly, the golden fusion of oppositions coexists with their brazen, unbridgeable dualities: "rud'st or gentlest sight," "most sweet favour or deformed'st creature," mountain or sea, day or night, crow or dove—each polar pair is seen as one, though (we are told) falsely through mystifying flattery, not truly through alchemy. All that his enraptured vision would bring together is yet left splintered and apart. Thanks to the errancy that accompanies a circumscribed and pointed affirmation—the dispersing shotgun now made companion to the piercing arrow—the newly transformed realities that the metaphor would create are undone in the creating.

The speaker, claiming exclusive control over the supervising voice of the poet, turning him into poet-lover with the lover's limitations as poet, sees each of his poems as seeking to become "the perfect ceremony of love's rite" (Sonnet 23). As a would-be religious rite, it insists upon the transformative metaphor that turns all into love, all into joy, all into the sacralized beloved—and does so through a reclaimed semiotic that "leaves out difference" and proclaims a three-in-one union. I refer to Sonnet 105, in which the three united adjectives, "fair, kind, and true" are, as in a liturgy, thrice pronounced, though the poet ends by confessing that—except in the extraordinary ritual that produced these poems—in the ordinary world the three "lived alone" and "till now never kept seat in one." And again we are left to see the words of the poem moving outward, away from its edges, to unweave the spectacular net—ever returning upon itself—that the poem-as-metaphor has sought to become.

> Let not my love be called idolatry,
> Nor my beloved as an idol show,
> Since all alike my songs and praises be
> To one, of one, still such, and ever so.
> Kind is my love today, tomorrow kind,
> Still constant in a wondrous excellence:
> Therefore my verse, to constancy confined,
> One thing expressing, leaves out difference.
> "Fair, kind, and true," is all my argument,
> "Fair, kind, and true," varying to other words;
> And in this change is my invention spent:
> Three themes in one, which wondrous scope affords.
> "Fair, kind, and true" have often lived alone,
> Which three till now never kept seat in one.

It is just this weaving and unweaving of the net of words that has made Ben Jonson's "Why I Write Not of Love" so precious a poem to me, since in it he explicitly sees the poet use this net—as the god Hephaestus had used his—as a way to entrap and hold and present the gods, and sees also the gods escape the net, forcing the words to de-sacralize themselves.

> Some act of Love's bound to rehearse,
> I thought to bind him in my verse:
> Which when he felt, Away (quoth he)
> Can poets hope to fetter me?
> It is enough they once did get

> Mars and my mother in their net:
> I wear not these my wings in vain.
> With which he fled me: and again
> Into my rimes could ne'er be got
> By any art. Then wonder not,
> That since, my numbers are so cold,
> When Love is fled, and I grow old.

Eros reminds the poet that Homer used his words to present the gods to their embarrassment, having Hephaestus forge the net in which he traps his unfaithful wife and her lover to display for the amusement of their fellow gods. But the binding net is clearly the poet's, as Eros knows, who uses it as his precedent to flee the present poem, thanks to his wings, not to be fettered again.

As the poet loses control over Eros, his words diminish from containers of the divine to empty counters: Love loses its substance as a human act as it loses its god, love fleeing with Love. The word *Love* loses its status as proper noun once it has lost Eros, and without the god and his Word the poet can only rejoin a loveless human history, and "grow old." He can write no longer of love since Love is fled from his poems, that net of his words, including the present poem that narrates the god's flight and its own consequent emptiness. Eros has been caught in this poem only to force it to chronicle his escape—from it and from all poetry. With the loss of its divinity, Love dwindles to love; but the latter cannot survive the diminution and vanishes with the emptying-out of the word that, forever lower-case, no longer contains its god—or any meaning, for that matter. The word loses its mystification when it loses its mythic substance.

My gloss on Jonson's poem furnishes the gloss on the title of this chapter: "The Figure in the Renaissance Poem as Bound and Unbounded." And it explains, in dealing with the poem's first two lines, why in that title I mix the two different, though related, verbs, *bind* and *bound* ("Some act of Love's bound to rehearse, / I thought to bind him in my verse"). "Love" in this poem is both conceptual noun and proper name: that is, as noun it seeks to bind the person of the god within its bounds to prove the legitimacy, the substantiality, of its meaning. And the poem itself, in the tradition of poets since Homer (who bound Hephaestus in his poem so that the latter could bind the divine lovers in *his* net), has sought to use words as a figural net to bind and bound a divine essence. But the closing of the net cannot prevent the escape of the elusive god, who escapes from (flees or bounds from) all bounds, all bindings, and makes a mockery of closure. Hence the folly of the poet's attempt to rehearse "Love's bound" by binding its divine embodiment in the poem. The verbal bond, with the verbal bound, is eluded by its would-be prey, who is unbounded by virtue of his being unbound. Hence the substantive *love*, by force of the poem's figural ambition, seeks to clasp its god within by a verbal power that displays its self-delusion. In the finality of that last bitter rhyme of "cold" and "old" ("That since, my numbers are so cold, / When Love is fled, and I grow old"), the poem completes itself, though only with the abandonment of its bereft speaker.

I have tried to show the duplicity at work in various forms of Renaissance metaphor in its figural pretensions, whether its quest for a sacralizing identity is stimulated by Mariolatry (identity between Mary and the beloved), by Christian typology (identity between historical individuals and the present beloved), or by classical myth (identity between the muse and the beloved, or between the heavenly goddess and the beloved, or between the classical god and the activity he represents). In each of these the metaphor, insofar as it is being viewed both as itself and as mock-metaphor, doubles itself and becomes a figure displaying four elements rather than just —as we should expect—two. As viewed from within the sacralizing figure, there are two elements that must be seen to fuse into the incarnating presence that obliterates the difference and distance between them. But, in stimulating our continuing awareness of that difference between the two, two other elements arise, each seeking to command the action at the expense of the other—never quite intermingling, never yielding ascendancy. Indeed, as in all allegory, there is a residue of inappropriateness as we apply the action to either, sensing it to belong exclusively to the other. In this second, de-sacralizing mode the interplay between tenor and vehicle in the metaphor (or mock-metaphor) makes the two both interchangeable and mutually exclusive. We may not know which is which, since we seem able to read both ways, but we are convinced of their distinctness, that neither can become the other. As our focus alternates from one to the other and back again, the disjunction between them is not bridged: with the poem's surreptitious encouragement, we do not stop comparing the two elements, so that we cannot overcome our sense of their incommensurability. It is just such an overcoming that the first, sacralizing mode requires. And this mode, for all its totalizing character, continues to be sustained as well, with all the force that the speaker's inner vision has realized in its language.

So what we have, as we pursue both modes, which continually double back upon one another, is—in effect—four elements, one pair functioning within the urge toward metaphorical fusion and the other pair, as if in mockery of the first, functioning within the urge toward a mutual exclusion that seems metonymic. Yet we do well to sustain both pairs, seeing each as the shadow seeking a reality that would efface the other. I concede that these are not really four elements, but only two that I am asking you to consider in two very different ways. My point is that the two are so changed in the move from the metaphoric to the allegorical (or counter-metaphorical) mode that they become other than they have been, and we may do well—analytically—to think of them as four to mark the extremity of this difference.

I can now summarize my argument. In the Renaissance the profane love poem that would sacralize its materials may borrow its metaphoric form from the language of Christian mystery that would literalize the metaphor; but we find the poem conceding that this process of adaptation carries with it a difference that counters the attempt to confer identity. And that concession turns the metaphor against itself. Its companion mock-metaphor multiplies into four the two elements of the original, literalized metaphoric form, reducing the transcendent realm to the dimensions of an unraised human history while cherishing that realm still, as if its profane materials had earned the right to claim it for its own. Consequently, the

metaphoric and mock-metaphoric directions double back on one
another, moving back and forth, here suppressed and there re-
appearing.

The Renaissance poet, in his shrewdness as poet, usually took his
Neo-Platonism as only half a commitment, though it offered to his
language a total and totalizing dream. In the Renaissance even more
than in other times, Platonism seemed to wear two faces, and opposing faces. One is lit up with the warmth of the human world in
which it is immanent, and the other austerely turns away from that
lowly world that it, as transcendent, contemns. The first lives com-
fortably with a monism; the second insists on the separateness of a
dualism with one half of that dualism rejected. It is easy enough to
trace a semiotics from each of these: the first—what we recognize
as a self-mystifying Neo-Platonism—is father to organicism and to
the literal reading of metaphoric identity in the union of a mutual,
sanctifying presence. The second celebrates a chasm of difference
that is not to be overcome, the dualistic division that we might
relate to a Protestant vision—or, for that matter, to the flourishing
of Ramistic logic in the sixteenth century. It would keep the earthly
on the ground and not permit it to be invaded and set aglow by that
which would bring it beyond itself to the heavenly. Words would
stay each within its own bounds and not violate the property of
other words and, thereby, the sensible propriety of verbal behavior.
Texts could not reach beyond a clean allegory, with each of the two
sides kept within its proper limits.

One might find in this second version the force of demystifying
arguments that still in our day argue for metonymic distinctness in
the movements of language. Those arguing today for the unaggran-
dizing, metonymic character of language would eliminate the transcendent heavenly realm of faith, but this difference does not affect
the semiotic since, for the dualistic pious Platonist, neither the
sensible world nor its language could presume to capture the transcendent. From Plato to Augustine and beyond, the intelligible
reality was not to be penetrated by, or to penetrate, the materials of
sense. As Kierkegaard reminds us, for such thinkers our worldly
realm, including its verbal representation, is the same before and

after the leap of faith to a transcendent entity that redeems that realm without, however, making itself visible (that is, present) within it. So the semiotic operation would be the same whether a transcendent realm is affirmed or denied, since language in either case is to resist any mystification that would bring the word beyond itself.

Perhaps out of his fealty to his language as a more ambitious instrument, the Renaissance poet did not usually commit himself to so disabling a dualism. Thus the apparent invocation of a Neo-Platonic monism that called for interanimation among words and worlds. But he is also too aware of the profane character of his mission not to undercut that invocation, as I have already argued. And, aware of the dualistic alternative—which, after all, is the apparently sensible way language would appear to operate if we did not mystify it—he introduces it as a mocking shadow to the metaphor he appears to maintain. So his poetic trick—because his poem is a special language game—permits him to put forth both at once, the closed and the open, metaphor and mock-metaphoric metonym, the spatial and the temporal, the immanent and a self-effacing transcendent, in a form whose organicism (or rather proto-organicism since organicism is not yet an enunciated doctrine) would reveal its own limits, its own dependence on the ever-opening character of language. The realm of belief (even the sacrilegious belief based on the sanctification of profane objects) accompanies the organic pretense in language, but both the organic in language and the sanctified in belief are broken apart as the words themselves force us to confront the discrepancy hidden within them in their pretensions. Language as discrepancy, and from there to metaphor as mistake. Still, there they stand—both language and metaphor—not altogether deserving our disbelief.

My summoning of Coleridge by invoking his use of "disbelief" —or rather by invoking his rejection of "disbelief" or at least suspension of it—is meant to prepare us for the movement that makes organicism an explicit doctrine, so that I may examine the extent to which openings can be made there too. As we have seen, there is not a well-formulated Renaissance theory to enunciate what Renaissance poems implicitly tell us of the complex semiotic that empowers them. (Indeed, well-formulated Renaissance theory would simply suggest a one-sided semiotic of the dualistic sort.) I have dealt in this essay not at all with explicit theoretical statements since they run pretty much in the wrong direction, if we are willing to see the poems working as I have been suggesting they do.[8] So we have to look elsewhere to find a theory that itself wants to speak this way for poetry.

I will turn in my next chapter to those in the late eighteenth and nineteenth centuries who take up the theoretical possibilities offered by organicism and try to follow them where they lead, even—as it sometimes seems—to logical extremes that seem self-defeating. However, I will—as you must suspect—try to find that, in spite of our most common readings of them, they often retain the awareness we have seen in their medieval and Renaissance poet-precursors that organicism, like any claim to verbal union, is a metaphor, one that, because of its limits as metaphor, announces its own mock-metaphoric counterthrust. And the mock metaphor, once grasped, must turn the metaphor inside out, though we are shocked to observe that, even inside out, it retains the same shape.

In the midst of this melange of mystification and demystification within these poems, there is nostalgia, which is the other side of skepticism. That is, there is among these poets a will to idolatry—indeed the forms of idolatry are being admiringly imitated as well as parodied—because the contemporary alternative to idolatry, with its claims to presence and transcendent identities, is a world of commonsense, businesslike distinctions that the poets find abhorrent.[9] These poems have been expressing all these incompatible attitudes and yet express also the possibility of holding together all that is so explosive within them—and us.

The poetic act represents the failure of the period ideology to sustain the enclosure it would enforce. Instead the poetic act probes to find the fissures of disbelief and slips in to explore and exploit them. It opens outward to the places where personal skepticism joins commitment in a carnival of language play celebrating the uncertainties it seeks to represent. And what had been a secure structure of linguistic hegemony is shaken and left tottering—or crumbled. Yet, unlike ideology, the poem itself stands up despite all its underminings, only strengthened by the cracks in its surfaces and depths. The well wrought urn should rather be thought of as the well cracked urn, its substance flowing through it until one cannot tell what is inside from what is outside: the world becomes its language and its language becomes the world. But it is a world out of control, in flight from ideology, seeking verbal security and finding none beyond that promised by a poetic text, but always a self-unsealing poetic text.

NOTES

1. Gombrich, for example, continually uses perceptual psychologists to support his claims. See, as just one instance, his essay in the collection of joint work in psychology and art criticism, *Illusion in Nature and Art,* R. L. Gregory and E. H. Gombrich, eds. (London: Gerald Duckworth & Co., Ltd., 1973).

2. I discuss the history of this distinction at length in my essay, " 'A Waking Dream': The Symbolic Alternative to Allegory," in *Allegory, Myth, and Symbol (Harvard English Studies 9)*, Morton W. Bloomfield, ed. (Cambridge: Harvard University Press, 1981), pp. 1–22.

3. *The Statesman's Manual, The Collected Works of Coleridge, Lay Sermons,* R. J. White, ed. (London: Routledge and Kegan Paul, 1972), p. 30.

4. There is, of course, the fourfold allegorical scheme, often cited from Dante to Northrop Frye, which is sometimes seen as an outgrowth of a more basic threefold, as argued in the instructive essay by Karlfried Froehlich, " 'Always to Keep the Literal Sense in Holy Scripture Means to Kill One's Soul': The State of Biblical Hermeneutics at the Beginning of the 15th Century," in *Literary Uses of Typology from the Late Middle Ages to the Present,* Earl Miner, ed. (Princeton: Princeton University Press, 1977).

5. *The Classic Vision* (Johns Hopkins Press, 1971), pp. 105ff. I pursue the notion of "metonymic metaphor" and relate it to "The Rape of the Lock" in *Theory of Criticism* (Baltimore: Johns Hopkins University Press, 1976), pp. 195ff.

6. I hope it is evident that I use "duality" in opposition to "unity" to signify the divided consciousness we associate with metonym in contrast to metaphor, while I use "duplicity" to signify that equilibristic process that leads us to sense a unity despite the evident duality (as in the mock-heroic) or to sense a duality despite the evident unity (as in the Renaissance mock-metaphor).

7. I am alluding here to a remarkable essay by Walker Percy that appeared as early as 1958: "Metaphor as Mistake," *Sewanee Review,* (Winter 1958), 66: 79–99.

8. I deal at greater length with the discrepancy between explicit Renaissance theory and the theory implicit in the poetry in "Poetic Presence and Illusion I: Renaissance Theory and the Duplicity of Metaphor," *Poetic Presence and Illusion* (Baltimore: Johns Hopkins University Press, 1979), pp. 3–27.

9. See "The Conversion from History to Utopia in Shakespeare's *Sonnets,*" *Words about Words about Words: Theory, Criticism, and the Literary Text* (Baltimore: Johns Hopkins University Press, 1988), pp. 242–55. There I make some social-historical suggestions about the grounds for these attitudes.

CHAPTER TWO

THE TYPOLOGICAL IMAGINATION AND ITS OTHER
FROM COLERIDGE TO THE NEW CRITICS AND BEYOND

> The reader should be carried forward, not merely or chiefly by the mechanical impulse of curiosity, or by a restless desire to arrive at the final solution; but by the attractions of the journey itself. Like the motion of a serpent, which the Egyptians made the emblem of intellectual power; or like the path of sound through the air;—at every step he pauses and half recedes, and from the retrogressive movement collects the force which again carries him onward. *Praecipitandus est liber spiritus,* says Petronius most happily. The epithet, *liber,* here balances the preceding verb.
>
> S.T. Coleridge,
> *Biographia Literaria,* Ch. 14

> Any "Socratic" method in criticism, if carried far enough (not very far, actually), reaches its limits and subverts itself.
>
> J. Hillis Miller,
> "Stevens' Rock and Criticism as Cure, II"

IN MY OPENING CHAPTER I traced the development of what I am calling the typological imagination, as well as its skeptical underside, through the duplicitous impact of the Renaissance metaphor. And I traced a connection from that metaphor, with its Christological sources, to romantic organicism by way of Coleridge, whose crucial distinction between symbol and allegory—I remind you—is for him intertwined with his theoretical instructions for interpreting the Sacred Book.[1] It is this association that leads Coleridge to convert his terms for the reading of the sacred text into guides for the reading of profane texts. The poem, as an imitation of the Bible's way of meaning, is to move the reader to respond to its language system as if to the Bible's.

Coleridge's valorization of the symbol, at the expense of allegory, rests upon his desire to have us read man's word as God's Word, a word imbued with the immanent presence of its meaning. Hence, when he comes to define the imagination, sublime agent of the poem as symbol, he treats it as a human imitation of the divine Genesis ("a repetition in the finite mind of the act of creation in the infinite I AM").[2] This call for the semiotic ideal and, consequently, for interpretive perfection would appear to be a prescription for closure of the sort I was trying to complicate and in part undermine in my initial essay.

The attempt to model our response to poems on the orthodox response to the Bible, the infallible and hence totally interpretable Book of Books, is in our own time projected into the hermeneutic framework proposed by Sigurd Burckhardt.[3] Burckhardt sets forth, as a fully self-conscious extreme, a theory of reading that fulfills the habit of interpretation which sacralizes all texts as if each were written by a poet-god in an act that is an imitation of Genesis.

Though working with ordinary words, despite the arbitrariness and contingency of their sound and the history of their meanings, Burckhardt's poet appears to the rapt (and trapped) reader to have converted the verbal structure into a network whose items have achieved an ontological status, so powerful is the claim to presence which they impose upon us. The reader, indulging the myth of total interpretation, must continue to sound each verbal note until he or she makes them all ring true. Or, to invoke Burckhardt's metaphor, the reader, refusing to rest in any *aporia,* must convert each "stumblingblock" to one interpretation that is no longer wholly satisfactory, into the "cornerstone" on which is founded a second interpretation that now appears more adequate. The one indispensable ground for this procedure is the assumption of the poem's infallibility, its total interpretability, like God's Book of Books, of which the poem is a microcosmic replica. Wherever an unexplained gap appears in the completeness of one's interpretation, it is up to the individual interpreter to accept that partial failure as his or hers and to refocus on the stumblingblock in hopes of finding a way to the completeness which, it must be assumed, the poem authorizes. The world of the poem is an undisrupted realm that celebrates an ultimate teleology. Here is a notion continuous with the Aristotelian doctrine of dramatic closure as well as with post-Kantian adaptations of the notion of "internal purposiveness," though the mystifying semiotic of Christian symbolism has given it new force because of the habits of figural interpretation it has imposed on poet and reader alike.

All of this, of course, is the furthest extension of the totalization that has exposed the organic tradition to the wide-ranging rejections of the past several decades. And it stems, I repeat, from the borrowing of the interpretive practices imposed by theological obligations associated with the reading of a sacred text. This borrowing, which authorizes how we are to interpret secular texts, is a larger reflection of the claim, made in my first essay, that poetic metaphor, as a breakthrough blurring—or rather fusion—of verbal entities, is a borrowing from our semiotic reading of the mystical identities forced upon the supplicant by Christian sacrament. But we also saw throughout that essay, beginning with my opening epigraph from Adorno, the secular need to de-sacralize the semiotic, but only while retaining the mystifying advantages of the sacred, even if always now as skeptics. (If I may repeat Adorno's words, "The profane secularizes the sacred realm to the point where the latter is the only secular thing left."[4]) What, in the typological tradition, we call the figural comes to be thought of as no more than figurative, though it does not appear to lose its semiotic pretensions.

The inherited pressures of our hermeneutic tradition encourage us to treat the figurative as if it still had the two-in-one identity of the *figura,* even as we accept our awareness of its diminished status. For the figural, as theologically—and hence typologically—sanctioned, was a figure that was substantively overdetermined, or rather predetermined, while in the figurative its secular character strips it of any substantive determination that would pretend to overwhelm its place in the realm of linguistic difference and allow it to bathe in a pool of substance that dissolves verbal distinctness. All this we would expect the secularly figurative to disdain in its insistence on not being predetermined (that is, on not being determined before the creative act of the poet), in its insistence on shedding its typological, its substantive burden, on being freely available for being put to any use. Still, the mystifications persist, as if the sanction of the sacred, via the figural, could be extended to the merely figurative. And the poetics of an unqualified organicism can be authorized only by such a confusion, which encourages it to literalize the metaphor in the borrowed manner of theological ritual, though now without a warrant to do so. For the organicist's semiotic presses secular metaphor itself into becoming the typological correlative of the sacred *figura*.

This literalizing of metaphor is in part the result of literalizing the metaphor of organicism itself, thrusting the biological fact of the organic outward into a universal existential projection which also serves as a single ontological ground. Further, the organic metaphor, converted into a universal figure, can, through its totalization, create the dangerous political consequences that have concerned many of its recent critics who move quickly to see the totalized as the totalitarian. As we have observed, for Coleridge himself aesthetics was inevitably intertwined with theology—and thus would have had political consequences. Organicists, true to their sources in German romanticism, too often project the organic metaphor—once literalized—into the realms of history and metaphysics, and use it to read the character of peoples, powers, and nations.

Thus converted into a hegemonic instrument, literary organicism can be uncritically analogized in order to serve as a justification for nationalism, for ethnocentrism even to the extreme of racism. We often witness—and are troubled as we witness—the wide-ranging indulgence in such unfortunate analogies here and there in Friedrich Schlegel, in Hegel, in Carlyle, later in Croce, and in several of those we still refer to as New Critics. The consequences of such analogies for reactionary twentieth-century ideologies have long been evident enough. Such political ramifications of the aesthetics of organicism might well arouse our suspicions about the other-than-aesthetic motives of those who developed this aesthetic that so quickly extended, via analogy, beyond aesthetics. In our own time suspicions of reactionary political motives, from Schlegel to Hegel to Carlyle and beyond, pursued the New-Critical organicists, who often encouraged these suspicions by their own political pronouncements. Indeed, the use of organicism to aestheticize the political, and hence to politicize the aesthetic, has for some time been a concern of enemies of organicism who have seen it—and rejected it—as an intrusive global claim. What then has followed is the condemnation of the entire realm of the aesthetic which, in its guise as organicist, is seen as harboring—and indirectly fostering—a repressive political agenda.

Of course, one may still worry that these analogies are at times too quick and easy for those who attack organicism, just as they are for those organicists who would use them to imperialize all the domains of thought and action. I have yet to be persuaded that the organic metaphor is *necessarily* dangerous in being applied to literary texts by other critics who, as secular skeptics, retain an awareness of the figurative, and even fictive, character of that application. More importantly, there are moments, as we shall see, when this self-consciousness—with the consequent half-disbelief that then accompanies the organicist rhetoric—invades, and thus qualifies, the critic's language, and renders it less invidious.

I want to suggest that we can find two perspectives—at some moments taken to be incompatible with each other, at more wishful moments proclaimed to be reconciled—throughout the more searching expressions of the organic metaphor. Or, to be less generous to what my claims here will be, let me say only that my re-reading of organic theory will claim to find support for its lasting legacy as a less restrictive legacy, one that has been foreclosed by those who dismiss organicists too easily, though I concede that they do so by taking them pretty much at their word, if too uncritically at their word. I want to suggest that there are movements in the texts of some of these critics that would guard against the dangers

implicit in organicist doctrine and would, instead, use it as a special
precaution against such excesses as those with which it is charged.

Such critics, concerned about the political consequences of an
imperialistic, global organicism that freely analogizes its claims, may
teach us (as I tried to do in my first chapter) to see in poems those
verbal workings that would disrupt what otherwise might be taken
as totalizing discourse—hardly poetic—that is the hegemonic imposition of an organically conceived historical moment. I would
urge that we see these more disruptive critics too as aesthetic organicists in their way, though they would use the aesthetic to subvert
the political as the dominant, rather than to reinforce it, and would
thereby claim a liberating, rather than a repressive, political function
for the aesthetic.

Yet today, newly sensitized as we are to find political rhetoric
everywhere, we are unlikely to resist the temptation to read across
from aesthetics to the realm of political power, insisting on spread-
ing the organic metaphor out, even when our authors might intend
it to be more modestly discrete. For example, when we read Coleridge
discussing the transformative "control" which the poet's imagination exercises over the materials furnished by his emotional life, we
come upon a forceful passage in which he refers to what was "originally the offspring of passion, but now [becomes] the adopted
children of power."[5] How insidious this may sound to some of us
today when the word "power" immediately arouses our recent sen-
sitivity to the language of politics. Or, when Coleridge speaks of the
"control" exercised by "the will and understanding" over the poet's
imagination, the word "control"—especially under the agency of
the will—can no longer be restricted to the disinterestedly aesthetic,
though Coleridge characterizes it as "gentle and unnoticed," even if
"irremissive."[6] Instead, it also tends today to be read as a term of
enforcement rather than—as the Coleridgean context suggests—a
term of endearment.

To what extent is that subtext of political enforcement already in
Coleridge's terms? His overcommitment to organic closure may
encourage today's readers to see the political there as an inevitable
accompaniment to its totalizing claim. Yet, as I sought to forewarn

you in my epigraph to this essay, there is in Coleridge—as in many organicists once they become self-conscious—another, and looser, more open side. It is as if he understands the need to leave an opening for the outside air that keeps the poetic system refreshed. The spirit of play and its consequent freedom, borrowed from Schiller's notion of "aesthetic education," introduces a lightness here and there in Coleridge's text and brings to mind the call for "variety," for the unfettered opening to "diversity," that everywhere accompanies the austere demand for "unity" in late eighteenth- and nineteenth-century organic theory.

Attacks on organicism too often suit the convenience of its antagonists by defining unity, and the form it characterizes, simply as a matter of an unruffled coherence in a given direction—not to be disturbed—with each particular detail serving the all-governing whole, indeed utterly subservient to it. The very language invites the political overtones of subservience and repression to intrude upon the aesthetic. But the issue is more complex for many organicists, and for the most interesting of them. Throughout the history of literary criticism in the West there has recurred a notion of "difficult beauty"[7] that has—in different ways and with different emphases—insisted on the paradox of a restrictive and yet capacious form, one whose restrictiveness can yet provide for that which would evade the restriction and threaten its very principle.

Though it is true that doctrines of literary form since Aristotle (for most of us the first organic theorist) depended on form's exclusionary power, the organic qualification required that it be pried open long enough to include the very elements that would undermine its principle of coherence as a totalized entity. Thus Aristotle may have continually pressed the need for probability, and hence for the uninterrupted logical coherence of an action, but only while insisting, and just as forcefully, that the element of surprise must also be introduced (by means of "recognition" and "reversal"), though at great risk to probability, in order to convert the "simple" plot to the "complex" plot.[8] The apparently disruptive must be intruded into, and yet made a necessary part of, a newly complicated pattern. In this way, life's unpredictabilities—even at times its im-

possibilities—must be accommodated by what would otherwise be
the too trim probabilities of art, though probabilities they must
remain. And in the struggle between that which fights for admission
and that which fights for form is the making of the great Aristotelian
poem. Indeed, greatness for him may well be measured by the
intensity of the struggle, by the resistance of the obstacles to an easy
system of probability, by the difficulty with which unity—and hence
poetic beauty—is achieved.

We find this struggle echoed in the more restless Renaissance
critics—like Jacopo Mazzoni, for example, who calls for the poet to
use his power of projecting the "phantastic" to intrude the "marvel-
ous" upon the merely "credible," using poetry to enlarge the domain
of what the reader finds believable.[9] Something of the same spirit
moves Dr. Johnson to forsake the neoclassical dramatic unities for
the expansive realm of theatrical make-believe and the "endless diversity" it can sponsor, once it seeks to include "the real state of
sublunary nature"—a "chaos of mingled purposes and casualties"—
rather than an artificially contrived selection from it.[10] At much the
same time Edmund Burke is generating a theory of the sublime to
bring a profound, disorderly challenge to the comfort of the undis-
turbed conformities of neoclassical beauty. And, beyond these, it is
Coleridge, in his discussion of Wordsworth's and his objectives in
the *Lyrical Ballads,* who seeks the problematic coexistence in poems
of "the charm of novelty," a "*sudden* charm" as if by supernatural
agencies, together with the familiar naturalness of everyday living.[11]
As he proceeds, he continually encourages the introduction into
poems of discordant elements that retard or even impede the imposition of the overall sovereignty of form.

Coleridge is yielding to this loosening of his organicist urge when
he introduces the motto he quotes from Petronius that is the heart
of my epigraph to this chapter: "*Praecipitandus est liber spiritus.*" He
approves of the balance struck between "*Praecipitandus est*" and
"*liber*": between being swept forward by the inevitabilities of organic form and yet maintaining the spiritual freedom that allows the
temporality of the journey to proceed with the leisure that allows its
momentary pleasures to be responded to. So the relation between

part and whole is not the austere, one-sided relation that organic closure might seem to dictate, with the first simply dependent on and responsive to the second. Instead, the part has an (almost?) independent *raison d'être* from one perspective (controlled by *liber*) even as, from another perspective (controlled by *praecipitandus*), it may be seen as contained by its function within the form of the whole. If I may again cite Coleridge's words, "the path of sound through the air," to which he is comparing the reader's passage through the poem, is hardly a metaphor for closure.

It is in the same mood that, in his discussion of the "irremissive, though gentle and unnoticed, control" of the poetic imagination by "the will and understanding," Coleridge uses another Latin motto, *"laxis effertur habenis,"* thereby again stressing the relaxed character ("loose reins") of the indulgence granted by that glorious unifying faculty as it carries itself onward. This is the relaxed character that allows the imagination to reveal "itself in the balance or reconciliation [or 'reconcilement'] of opposite or discordant qualities," a notion we might sum up by *"discordia concors,"* the phrase used by Dr. Johnson in the previous century to define "wit," the eighteenth century's pale equivalent of imagination. The first of the sequence of incompatibles that the Coleridgean imagination paradoxically balances or reconciles, a critic of today should be quick to note, is that "of sameness, with difference," an opposition that reminds us that we are again in the realms of metaphor and metonymy.

Although the emphasis is surely on the imagination's power of reconciliation, of producing unity in the face of opposition, that very power is dependent on the cultivation of that opposition, the indigestible food it must digest, but only by preserving our awareness of its resistance to being absorbed. Indeed, we must note again that Coleridge puts forth "balance" as an alternative to "reconciliation" ("balance *or* reconciliation"). But *reconciliation* and *balance* are not the same thing. *Reconciliation,* with the harmony of oppositions it imposes, is a synthetic Hegelian virtue, while *balance* suggests the maintaining of both the opposing elements at full strength, with neither yielding to the other. It is as likely to produce a tug-of-war in the observer as it is to produce the classic repose sought in the organicist's dream of totalized harmony. We will later see just this problem exacerbating the question of unity in I. A. Richards and the New Critics: can we depend upon the balanced opposition in "irony" or "tension" to produce an organized harmony and not an extended impasse?

It is, then, in the two-sidedness of this dialectic, with the opposition—especially the opposition between the would-be autonomous part and the would-be totalizing whole—being both indulged and overcome, that the aesthetics of organicism is made by Coleridge, and by those who follow him, to thrive. As I am describing it, built into the mystical dialectic of organicism, with its magical imposition of unity, is a negative thrust that would explode it. But it is a negative that the positive thrust—toward a miraculously closed union—depends upon cultivating as its antagonist in its ever-enlarging effort to encompass it. As we move through critics from Coleridge to the several New Critics, we find the emphasis sometimes on the ultimate closure, sometimes on the opening that struggles against being included; and, as we move through the nineteenth century into the twentieth, perhaps we find an increasing tendency to recognize the challenge of experience's infinite variety to the poem's desire to encompass it. But I am suggesting that in each case we find the requirement of closure accompanied both by the concern about the difficulty in accomplishing it and, despite such concern, by the desire for the poem to remain open provisionally to the assaults of new experience in the hope of domesticating them as well; though, once that is accomplished, as the dialectic continues, there is yet another assault, still another accommodation, etc., etc. The process goes on and on. Along with the anxiety to find closure, there is a companion anxiety *not* to yield to an exclusionary act that would end the process.

I have already suggested the extent to which the implied openings in Coleridgean organicism were consistent with Schiller's insistence on "play" as the middle agent reconciling the human instinct for form with the human instinct for incorporating the sensuousness of matter. In Kantian style, Schillerian play, hovering uncertainly between form and sense, reason and nature, is what makes the aesthetic possible even as an imperfect hope. But it is also what keeps the aesthetic open in the face of every attempt to close it off as an absolute system. Along with its reconciling mission, in its very freedom play must remain a destabilizing force, delicately teetering first one way, then the other, straining toward an equipoise that, as an idealized hope, could—if ever—be attained only for an instant before its obligation to be free would force it to move off once more, like Goethe's Faust obliged to flee the restful moment.

It is this restlessness, this continual need for movement, that keeps the post-Kantian versions of organic form from settling into the confinement that the more simple notion of closure propounded by those who would reject organicism would impose upon it. When, in the wake of Schillerian play, we turn to the several accounts of romantic irony proposed by German writers like Novalis, Friedrich Schlegel, Solger, and Tieck, we again observe the intrusion of a destabilizing element, provoking a trembling apprehension of uncertainty and doubling, a vain search for balance between an awareness of inside and outside that cannot with security know which is which. Nor can reflexivity be thus introduced without multiplying the perspectives and puncturing any would-be closure with diversions that defy the exclusions of formal unity.

Organicism's call for *unity,* it should now be clear, occurs only in the company of its opposite, the call for a *variety* that gives to any attempted unity a dynamics that threatens its stability. The absorptive power of any would-be unity must at every moment be challenged by that which would break it apart. To retain its dynamic character, it must cultivate its antagonist so that it may uncover always new and greater powers of accommodation. If this means it is always unsettled and in motion, then it is always in process, always working, as it should, in imitation of the continually proliferating energies of the natural order as a biological order: *natura naturans.* Here is the literalization of the organic metaphor in its most extreme form. But though this metaphor of organic nature, perhaps most insistently presented in Schelling's *Transcendental Idealism,* exposes the mystification of its aesthetic extension when it is applied to poetry, it also—on the other side—allows us to pursue the instabilities of a never-completed system always on the verge of remaking itself in response to the next threat to its momentarily achieved, precarious integrity. To borrow language from the epigraph I have taken from Hillis Miller, here indeed is criticism reaching its limits, but, in the very act of doing so, subverting itself.

In view of the increasing consciousness of temporality that accompanied the nineteenth century's obsession with evolutionary theory, it is not surprising that its contemporary arguments for organic unity represented an effort to force unity, as a spatial concept inherited from the neoclassical doctrine, to accommodate the shifting vagaries of time. But once those elements of experience are admitted which resist and would overwhelm the shapes of the merely spatial imagination, unity is never the same; indeed, it can be affirmed only while at the same instant being undone in the search for its continual reformulation by means of the struggle to encompass the ever-changing variety of the temporal. It is, I repeat, like that perfect moment which Goethe's Faust must continually resist even while he constantly strives to attain it.

This struggle between fixity and its unfixing by flux is delineated for modernism in the theory of Henri Bergson. Bergson charges the work of art to represent in a perceptible form the elusive temporal blur that defies form, paradoxically representing it in a form that somehow retains its elusiveness. This is to call for a form always in the process of disrupting its own pretension to closure in its ambition not to foreclose the fluid experience it seeks to represent. Outside the arts, Bergson would argue, discourse is content to serve its own closed ends by trimming experience to fit its own pragmatically restricted dimensions. But in the arts—and especially in the discursive art of poetry—Bergson finds the necessarily paradoxical desire to represent experience whose ever-changing contingencies resist representation. Any compromise for the sake of formal neatness would risk losing the honorific and privileged category of poetry. All claims to aesthetic closure must, then, be self-undermining if the contingencies of the temporal still—as they must—are to challenge the criteria for inclusion. Here in Bergson's metaphysic we find the systematic extension of that central oxymoron of romantic theory, unity-in-diversity.

This paradox is transmitted to the New Criticism by way of Bergson's English follower, T. E. Hulme, and its negative side, with its emphasis on the temporal, constantly insinuates itself and deflates the almost unlimited ambition of New-Critical claims for poetry. Its self-defeating terms render imperfect the analogy between the divine Book of Books and the individual earthly book on which the optimistic side of organicism depended. Indeed, it makes that comparison no more than a mock-metaphor, if I may recall this term from my first essay. The inconclusive inner struggle between unity and diversity, space and time, must lead to the concession that, while the double-edged typological *figura* of a divine creator might be said to straddle the domains of time and the timeless, it dwindles to the pretentious but limited *figure* in the language of a creature trapped within the unrolling incompleteness of human time.[12]

The New Criticism is inevitably associated with—and for some time has been inevitably condemned for—a positive organicism that calls for a total and totalizing functional unity as the overriding feature of the poetic text. But, as if following upon what we have already seen in earlier organicists, there is in the New Critics a negative side as well which runs counter to this common reading.

John Crowe Ransom himself, generally credited as the founder of the New Criticism and author of the book that gave the movement its name, spends much of his energy in his most influential work attacking a facile functionalism as part of the Hegelian holistic disease, whose totalizing consequences disturb him as much as they do many of the later detractors of the New Criticism. In the very essay that summarizes the argument of *The New Criticism*, he urges his anti-Hegelianism (which he elsewhere equates with an anti-Platonism) quite forcefully as the major poetic impulse.[13] He writes much in the spirit of Coleridge's concern—seen in my epigraph to this chapter—to preserve the *liber* and the *laxis* against being overwhelmed by the tight functional efficiency of a more austere and less complex notion of unity.

Ransom is willing—indeed is anxiously willing—to concede some independent pleasures of the text along the way and is not afraid to use a word like "arbitrary" (though probably with no awareness of the Saussurean tradition) or even "irrelevant" to describe the relation of meter or other poetic devices to the poem's meaning. Citing with approval the accumulation in the poem of "irrelevant *local* substance or texture" (my italics) as elements resistant to the "ruling idea" that would otherwise dominate the work (in compliance with the demands of Hegel's aesthetic, according to Ransom's antagonistic reading of it), Ransom attacks as anti-poetic those who would give any discourse, as a totality, an authoritarian—indeed tyrannical—control, over all its parts.

> They like to suppose that in poetry, as in chemistry, everything that figures in the discourse means to be functional, and that the poem is imperfect in the degree that it contains items, whether by accident or intention, which manifest a private independence. It is a bias with which we are entirely familiar, and reflects the extent to which our philosophy hitherto has been impressed by the successes of science in formulating laws which would "govern" their objects.

Like his phrase "ruling idea," the word "govern," placed in quotation marks by Ransom, indicates his awareness of the political metaphor buried in this language of domination and the poet's search for freedom from it: ". . . it was the political way of thinking which gave me the first analogy which seemed valid. The poem was like a democratic state, in action, and observed both macroscopically and microscopically." Obviously, for Ransom nonpoetic discourse is slave to the tyranny of Platonism, so that poetry achieves its license by allowing its elements the freedom to exercise a quasi-autonomy. And he wants the New Criticism to devote its energies to describing the "meanderings" in the verbal sequence that give the poem its richness without making them subject to the over-all pattern that would impose its control over them. For it is the particulars in the poet's "precious objects" (words chief among these objects, of course) that draw loving attention upon themselves and render them precious.

Thus it is that a thorough—and thoroughly positive—organicist like Cleanth Brooks quarreled with what he took to be Ransom's desertion of the cause, seeing him as lagging behind in his devotion to an outmoded, inorganic form-content dichotomy. Instead, it may well be that Ransom, dismissing the facile organicism that to him was represented by the simple model of political domination, was looking toward a more difficult and ambiguous relationship between part and whole, in which one cannot so easily determine what is or is not a meandering, or so easily dispense with the arbitrary, the local, and the apparently irrelevant. Indeed, in a curious but crucial passage that comes as a soaring conclusion to *The New Criticism*, Ransom seems to want both the free meandering of an independent—and independently precious—verbal moment and a new discourse founded on the specialness of this sequence of at once unbounded and bound moments.

In this passage (*The New Criticism*, pp. 314–16) Ransom begins by responding to the "powerful particularity" in the poem "which lurks in the 'body,' and under the surface of apparently determinate situations" and renders them less determinate. But this particularity, cherished for its own sake, somehow (and I use the "somehow" to emphasize the inexplicable, magical mystery of it all) becomes the enabling act for a new and expanded discourse, well beyond the reach of the trim, "logical" version that might find the particularity irrelevant. "In this way what is irrelevant for one kind of discourse becomes the content for another kind, and presently the new kind stands up firmly if we have the courage to stand by it." The "power of . . . positive particulars" hence transforms "indeterminacy of the bad sort."

This belated invocation suggests that Ransom in the end abandons the negative for what I have termed a positive organicism, so that the debate between him and Brooks is rendered moot. Still, in his anti-Hegelianism Ransom would insist that the independence of the part is not surrendered even in the newly achieved discourse. He clearly (or, really, not so clearly) wants to have it both ways. Such a double desire carries with it an unending tension between the need to admit the particularities arbitrarily seeking admission and the need to find a necessary and even indispensable role being performed by them after all. As with others in the organicist tradition, though in Ransom much more openly, we are being urged to perceive within the work conflicting elements that seek at once to control the particulars within it and to give them the freedom to challenge—indeed to threaten—its very definition as a single, integral entity. And Ransom is more anxious than his colleagues to allow the conflict to flourish because it is in the momentary, free gestures of language that he finds the specially liberating function of poetic discourse—as open—in contrast to the hopelessly closed submissiveness of prose discourse to the rule of its "Platonic censor."

Those New Critics who learned from Ransom were more uncomfortable than he with unresolved oppositions, with apparent loose ends, so that they sought more singlemindedly to fuse all resistant elements into an organic unity. And my own early work devoted to these critics, *The New Apologists for Poetry* (1956), pursued their organicist objectives at the expense of what then seemed like the more dualistic alternatives being persisted in by Ransom. I then saw these as Ransom's echoes of premodernist theories wedded to the form-content dichotomy rather than as foreshadowings of the postmodern appreciation of the arbitrary, the anti-systematic, the unabsorbed and unabsorbable. The shift in the relative weights I am now according the two nouns in the paradoxical phrase, unity-in-variety, or identity-in-difference—increasingly calling attention to the second (variety or difference) at the expense of the first (unity or identity)—is a reflection of what the intervening years have taught me about the intricacies of organicism. If in my early work I looked at the New Criticism only to find a positive organicism in it, so that I saw Ransom as a defector, I can see it from the other end now, as I have finally caught up to what Ransom was implicitly pointing toward.

Yet even those New Critics like Allen Tate or Cleanth Brooks, whom we think of as monistic—and hence more typical—in their hopes for the poem as interpretable object, make their momentary concessions to those hold-out forces seeking both to remain unabsorbed and to drive an opening in any entity that would accommodate them. For example, although Tate prescribes that the poet strive to achieve a unified state of "tension" in the poem that organizes all the stages of meaning in the poem from the "intensive" to the "extensive," from the literal to the figurative, the very notion of "tension" constitutes a continual threat to formal reconciliation and would counteract its very claim. Under its dominion the centrifugal is at every moment there to war with the pretended dominance of the centripetal. Tate's "tension" is an inheritance from I. A. Richards' doctrine that a poem is to create a balance or equilibrium among the reader's normally opposed impulses by means of its irony —except that, with Tate as with Richards, we may well resist being persuaded that, according to their theories, the several pulls of the poem will bring our impulses together rather than sustaining a continual struggle between them, each threatening to tear them apart.

I do not mean to underplay the extent to which organicism was indeed a totalizing concept for the New Critics as a group and for the New Criticism as a general analytic method. It would be a mistake to reduce the extent to which closure was their point of emphasis. Among them Cleanth Brooks offers the anti-organicist skeptic the most untroubled and apparently unqualified call for organic unity in the poem. His humanist claim assumes the conception of a pre-poem experience that is endlessly open, without form, and a poem, constructed out of elements of that experience, which yet transforms them into a closed text: ". . . the poet can make his poem *one* by reducing to order the confusions and disorders and irrelevancies of ordinary experience in terms of one unifying insight. . . . The poet not only *may* do this; he must."[14] Clearly this sort of poem must be closed to experience in order to keep from being contaminated by its confusion, disorder, and irrelevance. It is far more restrictive, cut off from human experience, than we saw Ransom's version of the poem, with its cultivation of irrelevancies, to be.

Yet even in Brooks we can find this one-sided emphasis under-

mined. As a single example, only a few pages earlier Brooks—
courting contradiction—not only seems to open the poem to experience but even treats it as itself a part of experience. He justifies the
fact that "poet after poet [chooses] ambiguity and paradox rather
than plain, discursive simplicity" because the "true poem is a simu-
lacrum of reality—in this sense, at least, it is an 'imitation'—by
being an experience rather than any mere statement about experience
or any mere abstraction from experience." Since experience is disorderly and confusing, only ambiguity and paradox can seek to repro-
duce it in words. Once more the resistance to the "one unifying
insight," the persistent provocation against it, is as indispensable to
the poet as is the attempt to impose that insight.

Brooks thus joins the others I have used to make up the long,
ambivalent narrative of organicism, those who—despite differences
of emphasis among them—hold their focus on the self-enclosing
text only while attending all that would expose it to the world, and
to the world of words, all that would bring the outside inside and
thus expunge any division between the two. It is Brooks' related
English colleague and yet opposite number among the New Critics,
William Empson, whose championing of ambiguity—in the shadow
of I. A. Richards—proposes a view of the poem as a shotgunning
of poetic meanings, with a dispersal much more emphasized than a
converging unity.[15]

I have already suggested the extent to which New-Critical organicists followed Richards' precedent in resurrecting romantic irony
and giving it a special role in blocking any singleminded poetic
response. From the moment he valorized the poem for "bringing in
. . . the opposite, the complementary impulses,"[16] Richards opened
poetic interpretation to an internal re-reading that was an undoing
of itself. The poem was thus freed to undermine any totalitarian
discursive intent, and theory was on its way to Ransom's use of a
political trope to grant to literature a democratic emancipation
whereby the errant part could resist the Platonic or Hegelian tyranny of the whole that imposed itself unchallenged outside the
literary realm. Theory is on its way also to the cherishing of irony,

ambiguity, and paradox we associate with Brooks and—might I
suggest?—to the point of closest contact between the New Criticism (once it has been purged of its commitment to a closure it
could not consistently sustain) and the species of deconstruction we
associate with Paul de Man. Yet it would not do to overplay the
concordant side of *this discordia concors* (between the New Criticism
and de Man) that I hardly dare propose in view of the fact that de
Man drew much of the power of his revisionary readings from his
rejection of the New Criticism.

One may suspect, as a result of recent disclosures of his early
wartime writings, that the strenuous anti-organicism manifested in
de Man's major work of many years may have been generated by his
intense, anxiety-driven revulsion against his succumbing as a juve-
nile to the dangerously unhealthy attractions of the nationalistic
political extension of organicism that I warned against earlier in this
chapter. To the mature de Man organicism was very likely a doctrine
limited to being the inevitable companion of dangerously totalitarian tendencies, a dehumanizing horror masked by the seductive
aestheticizing of the political. Whatever the cause, this consistent
antagonism to organicism—and to its corollary, the aesthetic—led
de Man to a radical re-reading of romanticism and its relation to
later nineteenth and twentieth-century criticism. That re-reading,
which takes its course by replacing Coleridge and his German sources
with de Man's version of Rousseau and Wordsworth, seeks to establish a tradition built out of a resistance to organicism and its totali-
zations, built out of a renunciation of the unifying power of language—now bereft of any aesthetic dimension—to overcome its
inescapable subversive moments. For moments were all that the
realm of language displayed.

De Man's continual and vehement rejection of an organicist romanticism rests, as I have suggested, on his own one-dimensional
reading of organicism that confines it to what I have called its
positive mode that presses for unity at all costs, without tolerating a
secessionist element. This may be a convenient reading to respond
to one's implicit political concerns about the extreme consequences

of a simplistic organicism, though it must overlook most of what I have been emphasizing about organicism's negative—its holdout—underside.

Even in de Man's partisan reduction of organicism, however, he acknowledges that a counter-organicist tendency emerges—at least by the time of the New Criticism—as if against the will of its practitioners, so that they wrongly assimilate it into their theory without understanding its implications.

> Is not this sense of the unity of forms being supported by the large metaphor of the analogy between language and a living organism, a metaphor that shapes a great deal of nineteenth-century poetry and thought? . . . As it refines its interpretations more and more, American criticism does not discover a single meaning, but a plurality of significations that can be radically opposed to each other. Instead of revealing a continuity affiliated with the coherence of the natural world, it takes us into a discontinuous world of reflective irony and ambiguity. *Almost in spite of itself,* it pushes the interpretative process so far that the analogy between the organic world and the language of poetry finally explodes. This unitarian criticism finally becomes a criticism of ambiguity, an ironic reflection on the absence of the unity it had postulated. (my italics) [17]

I of course agree with the discovery in the New Critics of a tendency to pursue centrifugal meanings even at the cost of their centripetal hopes for poems. Throughout these essays, however, I prefer to maintain that, from the early versions of organicism on, far from being an antagonistic intrusion, the *variety* side of the *unity-in-variety* motto is built into organicism's sense of itself and requires a fuller reading of it by us.

J. Hillis Miller adopts de Man's view of organicism and also attacks it in a way that, in the process, seems to concede its own ability to nourish its negative, shadow side: "The New Criticism discovered irony and the irresolvable ambiguities of figure. These discoveries subverted, at least implicitly, its presupposition that a poem is a self-contained 'object,' an organic unity." Earlier in this two-part essay Miller suggests he is speaking in the spirit of I. A. Richards when he claims that "the vocabulary of a poet is not a gathering or a closed system, but a dispersal, a scattering."[18] Indeed, as I have already suggested, Richards' immediate follower, William Empson, who is usually accepted as an early New Critic, produces his initial work in theory in accordance with such a claim.

I do not believe these are *ad hoc* "discoveries" (Miller's word) which the reading process, as an application of their theory, unexpectedly turns up to subvert the New-Critics' version of organicism, but rather that the theory itself solicits, encourages, and welcomes —indeed requires the critic to search for—such discoveries that break open closure and disrupt its comforts. For I have found this negative, shadow side inseparably present from the start as part of the dialectic that has given organicism its vital character, that has kept *it* open despite the more inflexible reading of it that would close it in and thus close it down.

Although I have been emphasizing the neglected underside of the organicist tradition, at no point in this chapter have I meant to deny the obvious fact that, from Aristotle to Kant to Coleridge to the New Critics, this tradition has pursued the integral unity of the work of art as its primary objective. From the biological model that shaped the poetics of Aristotle to the typological model borrowed from Christian interpretive practice by Coleridge and projected into a total mythic structure of interpretation by Burckhardt, there is a desire to have language overcome its differential character in order to partake of the identity of oneness. In Coleridge's desperate—and not always well advised—coinages of terms like "esemplastic" or "coadunative," invented by him to force his discourse to convey the sense of "many into one," we trace the repeated struggle in this tradition to find a critical language that might represent this verbal magic.

But as my initial chapter showed the sacrilegious betrayal of the typological model by its secular version, so throughout this essay I have introduced the skepticism that underlies the apparent pieties of romantic and modernist organicists. Their version of a would-be unified object requires that we see it as already opening itself to yet another disunifying element, the whole brawling mass constantly in motion, in a turmoil that is itself a process being at once overcome and regenerated. Thus the oneness of the text is a continually restless and, hence, endangered oneness, with an always about-to-be exploded tension between the desire to contain and the desire to include what cannot be contained, between the desire to represent and the desire for the unrepresentable.

I have no wish to deny that organicists—and the New Critics chief among them—readily invoke the language of ontology, with its mystifications, to ground their claims about the literary work as object. Despite their apparent metaphysical commitment, however, what is primarily being appealed to is the reading experience, a reading experience that is ever disturbed, ever reopening, ever self-challenging and hence self-renewing. It is this experience that was to be encouraged again and again not to rest in any momentary unified response, but to expose that response to fresh disturbances. Once thus disrupted, it would search anew for an interpretive unity and, after barely a moment of illusionary comfort, would admit—indeed would seek out—still another disruptive challenge. And interpretation of texts in our time—literary texts or ostensibly non-literary texts treated as literary texts—provides continuous evidence of the extent to which this encouragement has been heeded. The quest for interpretive unity—or, in these more self-conscious days, for instabilities that deny the possibility of unity—that quest never relaxes, never closes off the possibility of claiming new configurations: in the constant reopening of the text, commentators reopen both the particular interpretation and the interpretive process itself. For the interpretive unity being sought itself rests on the refusal to rest: it gives rise to its own antagonist in the very act of being defined, thereby unconfining itself.

One may question whether it is appropriate still to use the term *organicism* to cover the paradoxical attempt to loose the anti-unifying forces as a continual and risky challenge to what might otherwise have been thought of as at least a momentarily achieved unity. I would, in answer, suggest that—like the notion of metaphor in general—this use by theory of the metaphor of the organic must itself be subject to its own metonymic undoing. And nothing could be more appropriate for the most perceptive understanding of how organicism as a theoretical metaphor has functioned. Thus I have referred to narrower and broader characterizations of the organicist tradition, depending on the recognition of its negative as well as its positive thrust. And I again observe that it has been most convenient, for those who are anxious to dispense with the word and its tradition altogether, to read it narrowly, as if the metaphor were to be taken literally and only literally, as an uncritical self-mystification, and not in the duplicitous way that the profounder versions of this tradition themselves sanction.

The illusion of closure, of the centripetal insistence of our attentiveness, contains, *for our moment of perception,* those divergent, centrifugal forces that would carry us into the uncontrollable instabilities of timebound human experience, with all its contingencies, which make all representations of them seem tamely reductive. I might have used, as the most obvious metaphor of this paradox of representation, the illusion afforded by the proscenium-bound stage, contained by its arch and by the finalities of the last line of the fifth act. And yet the action onstage is strangely responsive also to the unpredictabilities of the intruding world of "real" happenings and other texts beyond its frame: the closed fable onstage and the open experiences that feed it. It gives us the chance both to grasp at the dream of identity—the realm of archetypal characters in an absolutely integrated and transfixed action, a model of teleology—and to be roused by the waking exposure to the ruthless, daylight language of the distinction-ridden business of our own living. Yet it is the co-presence of the demystifying act that permits us to entertain this dream, which is created only as it is exposed to the continuing threat of demystification.

Of course, the outside "reality" that the dramatic representation admits in order to negate it is only one more, routine discourse that we have carried with us into the theater, anticipating its dislocation by the spectacle at hand. Yet as the external alternative to the controlled contours we enter, it may, by way of contrast, well appear as an unformed chaos. But it is only a fictional "other" invented by the organicist's aesthetic need in order to explain or even to believe in the literary fiction at hand as a fully formed creation beyond a "given," which, as preformed or as preceding this literary form, may be taken to be that chaos beyond.

Clearly a post-Kantian (or at least a post-Burkean) notion, this disorderly "outside" is reintroduced—since the late eighteenth century—as the sublime, always the disruptive threat to the beautiful. Indeed, it is the potential intrusions upon the trim dimensions of the beautiful by the unleashed force of the sublime that unsettles and deepens theories of organic form after Kant as I have described them here. Recently the work of Jean-François Lyotard, which re-reads Kant's sublime with postmodern eyes, turns to important social-political uses the breaking up of unified, orderly structures, of master narratives, by the miscellaneous "little stories" that remain autonomous, unadaptable. Here, with arguments that carry forward Bakhtin's dialogical battle—with heteroglossia and carnival as his instruments—against any generic or aesthetic domination, Lyotard's becomes a later and surely more negative version of that complex organicism (with its correlative anti-organicism) that I have traced through the nineteenth century to its explicit articulation in Ransom's call for textural "irrelevance" and its almost autonomous character. The postmodern sublime and its splintering of a totalizing doctrine of drama—its scattering of the enclosed stage—far from being discontinuous with earlier theory, is rather an extreme expression of what was recurrently, if at times inaudibly, a dissonant, and dissident, note within it. Understanding this, we better understand Lyotard's continual invocation of Kant (if not Edmund Burke), though it is now a Kant forced anachronistically to defy his chronological place.

In effect, as an allegory of literary works at large, the double reality of the stage and its action—the competitive co-presence for the audience of both the contoured stage and the unabsorbed word-world beyond—functions as a typological figure in much the manner of the metaphor in the Renaissance lyric, as I examined it in my first chapter. The totality of our commitment—in a metaphor as in a dramatic character—to the single and absolute presence of a fused signifier-signified coexists with a secular skepticism, a recognition of contingency that demystifies it into differentiated dualities. The two semiotic systems, so mutually antagonistic, constantly redispose themselves and one another, even to the apparently impossible point of being mutually supportive. Distinctions thus undo themselves: inside can be seen as outside, the closed can be seen as open, the open as closed. Every direction can be seen as a two-way street. Which way can one face when every face appears as Janus? To establish the power of this Janus paradox and to treat it as a power used by the reader to see the literary work as a probe of fictional and existential identity, these will be the concerns of my third chapter.

NOTES

1. I refer again to *The Statesman's Manual, The Collected Works of Coleridge, Lay Sermons,* R. J. White, ed. (London: Routledge & Kegan Paul, 1972), p. 30.
2. *Biographia Literaria,* chapter 13.
3. In "Notes on the Theory of Intrinsic Interpretation," *Shakespearean Meanings* (Princeton: Princeton University Press, 1968), pp. 285–313.
4. "On the Relation Between Art and Society," *Aesthetic Theory,* trans. C. Lenhardt (London and New York: Routledge & Kegan Paul, 1984), p. 8.
5. *Biographia Literaria,* chapter 18.
6. *Ibid.,* chapter 14.
7. The phrase "difficult beauty" is an important one in Bernard Bosanquet's *Three Lectures on Aesthetic* (London: Macmillan, 1915).
8. *Poetics,* chapters 9 and 10.
9. "On the Defense of the Comedy of Dante," in *Literary Criticism: Plato to Dryden,* Allan H. Gilbert, ed. (New York: American Book Company, 1940), pp. 360, 370–71, 388.
10. "Preface to Shakespeare," in Samuel Johnson, *Selected Prose and Poetry,* Bertrand H. Bronson, ed. (New York: Rinehart & Company, 1952), especially pp. 245, 261.
11. *Biographia Literaria,* chapter 14.
12. Guy Sircello reminds me that we must not neglect the important contribution of John Dewey's systematic balancing and interfusing of the closed and the open, the static and the dynamic, the spatial and the temporal, in his strikingly prophetic work, *Art as Experience* (New York: Minton, Balch, & Co., 1934).

See, among many places in that seminal book, "The Act of Expression," pp. 58–81.

I must record here my own indebtedness to that book, which had its effect on me well before I wrote *The New Apologists for Poetry* (1956), when I first read it and wrote on it under the tutelage of Eliseo Vivas, who also claimed to have learned substantially from it. But I believe it is only in my present undertaking that the full force of Dewey's ever-opening dialectic is reflected. Recent developments in the work of fellow theorists make it clear that it is not in my work alone that Dewey's relevance is currently being revived.

13. "Criticism as Pure Speculation," in *Critical Theory Since Plato*, Hazard Adams, ed. (New York: Harcourt Brace Jovanovitch, 1971), pp. 881–890. The quotations in the discussion that follows appear on pp. 887 and 886, respectively.

14. *The Well Wrought Urn* (New York: Reynal & Hitchcock, 1947), p. 203. The contrasting quotation in the next paragraph appears on p. 194.

15. In *Seven Types of Ambiguity* (London: Chatto & Windus, 1930).

16. *Principles of Literary Criticism* (London: Routledge & Kegan Paul, 1925), p. 250.

17. "Form and Intent in American New Criticism," collected in *Blindness and Insight* (New York: Oxford University Press, 1971), pp. 27–28. De Man's attack on the organicist defense of the symbol, as represented by Coleridge and those who are influenced by him, takes a later form in "The Rhetoric of Temporality," in *Interpretation: Theory and Practice,* Charles S. Singleton, ed. (Baltimore: The Johns Hopkins Press, 1969), pp. 173–209.

18. The first of the quotations appears in "Stevens' Rock and Criticism as Cure, II," *Georgia Review* (1976), 30:345. The second appears in Part I, "Stevens' Rock and Criticism as Cure," *Georgia Review* (1976), 30:7.

CHAPTER THREE

STRICKEN
BY METAPHOR
SOME THEMATIC CONSEQUENCES

I dug in the quiet earth and wrought the tomb
And made these lines to memorize their doom:
Equilibrists lie here; stranger, tread light;
Close, but untouching in each other's sight;
Mouldered the lips and ashy the tall skull,
Let them lie perilous and beautiful.

John Crowe Ransom,
"The Equilibrists"

IF I MAY THEMATIZE the consequences of the indulgence in metaphor, I can ask, what are the risks inherent in the figuralism produced by the typological imagination when it is carried over into the secular word? In my first chapter I observed in the Renaissance both the habit of literalizing the secular adaptations of Mariolatry or other Christian transfigurings and the poet's wariness that put him on guard against the threat of the magical semiotic even as he indulged it. Thus even the poets celebrating the possibilities of secular love felt the need to open metaphor up to the skepticism of difference, though only while their typological imagination dwelled on the power of poetic language to produce identity.

According to the usual formulation in old rhetorical primers instructing us in the use of figures of speech, it is by the removal of "like" or "as" from between the two substantives being compared that a simile turns into a metaphor ("My love is like a rose" into "My love is a rose"). And there is a discursive—eventually an ontological—universe of difference between the two. In the simile the elements in the two entities are laid out side by side, and those that are similar separated from those that are different. (I say elements that are "similar" rather than those that are the "same" because the awareness of difference keeps the two substantives apart even in the moments of likeness.) The two entities barely touch and hardly overlap. In the metaphor, on the other hand, the copula bestows equivalence: one substantive is seen *as* the other, the one wholly absorbed into the other (with the very opposition between oneness and otherness obliterated) in the drive to overwhelm difference in the pressure toward utter identity. The metaphor, in other words, would perform a small act of transubstantiation. Once stricken by it, we have an enlarged, newly created verbal fusion in which oppositions are reconciled—or, to put it less favorably, entities are utterly confused.

The poet is authorized in metaphor to function as this lesser god in theories of poetry from the French Symbolists—if not from Coleridge—through the New Critics. For them the task of the poem is to become a metaphor or self-sufficient "symbol," to perform the transubstantiating act and make it stick. It is to seal us within the transforming moment of vision, enclosing one substantive exclusively under the aegis of another, in effect excluding difference itself from the realm of discourse, the realm in which difference usually functions and which, through that function, it controls. This mystifying movement beyond difference is perhaps climaxed in Northrop Frye's scheme where, as the highest and ultimate level, the "anagogic" phase absorbs the others as it dissolves all distinctions into the world (and the world of language) as symbol, as metaphor, as identity: "the still center of the order of words" "in which everything is potentially identical with everything else." That this is a totalizing act of closure is at once evident in Frye's title for his anagogic phase: "Symbol as Monad."[1] Here is the farthest reach of the excesses laid at the door of organicism, and for good reason.

But I have argued that organicism can be something more—or rather something less—as well, since, once it pursues its own restless contradictions, it can also turn this totalization inside out. And we are reminded of the mistake into which the metaphor would lead us if we should take its illusion as a claim to an actually changed reality; if, in other words, we should yield to the deception that Frye himself calls "existential projection."[2] It was to find an implicit concern about this mistake in even the most ambitious claims of organicists that my second essay was directed. Led on by the typological imagination, aesthetic organicism can itself be stricken by metaphor—both by the notion of metaphor as transubstantiating and by itself (organicism) as metaphor. But at its best (which for me is to say at its most self-conscious) it recognizes the malady, in part recovers, and retreats from its excesses. To allow oneself to be stricken by metaphor without recognition, recovery, and retreat is —as we shall see—to rest in a state of danger.

It was as a reaction against the more extravagant claims of organicism, which were typically—if not quite accurately—taken to be the whole of organicism, that deconstructionist theorists, of whom in the United States the most striking was de Man, asserted the function of difference as a persistent and irrepressible function, thereby converting every would-be metaphor into a self-disruptive metonymic sequence, every would-be symbol into a series of allegories. These would remind us of the inevitable failure of language as an instrument of representation, so that the momentary illusions created by a poem's verbal enclosures, once revealed as no more than illusionary, as only fictional, open up the very discourse they would seal off.

The leap to identity from difference, the leap to metaphor from simile—from the common sense of metonymy—is an existential leap as well as a verbal leap, a leap probably not unrelated to Kierkegaard's leap of faith, although the claim here is that poetry enables language to represent that leap, as is not the case in Kierkegaard, for whom the leap cannot be charted by signs. Similarly, the rejection of that leap as a poetic possibility—the need to bring it to earth—depends on a skeptical conviction of what language can*not* do as an instrument of representation of the "real" as well as what it cannot do as an internalized system of differentiations. This rejection, like any hardheaded denial of leaps, also carries existential accompaniments with it. These are the thematic consequences to which I mean to call attention as this essay develops.

The aim of my initial chapter was to add the shrewd doubleness and self-skepticism of secular metaphor—its awareness of itself as mistake even as it would enforce itself toward self-enclosure—to add this doubleness to the singleminded mystifications of the theological commitment and the all-affirming leap it authorizes. And my second chapter intended to find a theoretical grounding of this added awareness in what is otherwise seen as a less complicated organicist tradition. The fictionalizing of the metaphorical move toward identity and—even more—the apparent self-consciousness with which that fictionalizing act is performed, these insure the poem against that "existential projection" of the mimetic fiction that Northrop Frye warned poetry and its critics to resist. Such warnings come to us still shaped by Matthew Arnold's earlier warning, echoed for modernism by I. A. Richards, that literature, as the secular substitute for religion, was to engage the realm of belief only by disengaging it from any claim to being grounded in fact. This was to be its safeguard against being dissolved (our word would be "deconstructed") because, as had already happened with religion, the fact—as scientific fact—had failed it.[3]

This secular role that is assigned to poetry attributes to it a reflexive shrewdness that guards our modernist giants against any extravagance that is unchecked by the simultaneous sense of what undermines it. It is what differentiates Shelley, with his self-convinced rapture, from a self-doubting religious poet like T.S. Eliot even in his moments of theological zeal. Even in these moments Eliot, unlike Shelley, sees language, and *his* language, as breaking because it cannot bridge the way to the presence of the unbroken *one* it must see itself as striving to become. In the *Four Quartets* the poet finds his words repeatedly falling away from what they must join. "Words, after speech, reach / Into the silence" in an effort—through "form," through "pattern"—to "reach the stillness." However, "Words strain, / Crack and sometimes break, under the burden, / Under the tension, slip, slide, perish, / Decay with impreci-

sion, will not stay in place, / Will not stay still."[4] These words
resemble Becket's acts and the incomplete way in which they do and
do not represent saintliness in *Murder in the Cathedral*.[5] Or in *The
Cocktail Party* we have the ironic enactment of the metadramatic
allegory of the playwright's control in Harcourt-Reilly's mock-mas-
tery of the play's action. This action, after the report of the absurd
mock-crucifixion of Celia Coplestone, concludes only with the prep-
aration for a party about to begin—or begin again. The action has
been controlled by the psychiatrist as internal playwright only to
escape him into an uncontrollable, ever-opening infinite regress. It
is as if one of our last great modernist poets, for all the religious
desperation of his quest for tradition and its authority, is turned
into (or rather turns himself into) an early postmodern who recognizes closure as the poet's illusion. His is not altogether unrelated to
Serenus Zeitblom's vision, in Mann's *Doctor Faustus*, of Adrian
Leverkühn's relation to the closures of the classically modernist
musical tradition: Zeitblom sees Leverkühn as representing a finality
that explodes what it can complete only in the act of destroying it.

Consequently, that total enclosure by metaphor (to be avoided),
which would be undone by an exclusively skeptical awareness that
the metaphor is a mistake (also to be avoided), uneasily relaxes into
our double sense of both the metaphor *and* its mistakenness. The
counter-metaphorical consciousness of language's continuing incompleteness keeps us open to the differential realm beyond metaphor even while we feel ourselves within its enclosing verbal power.
Our grasp by the metaphor must survive its reintroduction as simile,
which returns us to that in the comparison between the two entities
which falls short of bringing them together as one, that which keeps
them two and different. Still, despite our skepticism about the
presumption of metaphor, our grasp by it must also survive.

In these chapters I have been allowing metaphor to stand for the
several ways in which we encourage the poem to work its magic
upon us, persuading us toward the dream of identity with its presence and presentness, where we should have expected to find only
difference with its distances in space and time. As I have suggested
before, the thematics of this opposition between sameness and dif-

ference, metaphor and metonymy, achieves a climactic self-consciousness in de Man's work, especially his earlier work, which is all
on the side of metonymy and embattled against metaphor. My
entire career, on the other hand, may be seen as an attempt to make
a credible case for the verbal presence of metaphor in poems, whatever the thematic gaps, the absences, it covers, and by covering
manages to reveal.[6] But I desire the verbal absolute of metaphor in
the face of metonymy only while acknowledging the need in poems
for each to carry the sense of its becoming its other, continually
carrying out the paradox of a polarity in which the poles become
identical without yielding up the opposition of their mutual exclu-
sivity.[7]

It should be evident—and I readily concede—that many verbal
instances outside those texts we denominate as poems can work
upon us in this way, appearing to fight for identity while retaining
the awareness of difference. And, poems or not, we can read them
as participating in such textual duplicity. We distinguish their verbal
strategy from the less resistant strategy of would-be transparent texts
that succumb to difference, or that seek it, though even such texts
may be seen as occasionally slipping, through a kind of blindness,
into that which would blur differences. To stumble unwittingly into
the blindness of a language whose meanings overrun one another,
however, is perceived as hardly the same as the activity that cherishes
and plays with such verbal perversity. I concentrate upon poems,
then, because it is in them—in writing them and in reading them—
that the duplicitous strategy can most readily be perceived as thriv-
ing, indeed as being exploited.

To the extent that we encourage poems to work upon us, we
encourage a magical conversion that would permit the union of
word and thing, or of word and word, or—in narrative—of character and character, of action and action. That is, it would permit
the word to realize the dream of total representation, appearing to
sweep disparate things into its newly substantive oneness; or it may,
as we saw in the Renaissance, permit disparate words to fuse in
sound and meaning; or it may permit disparate characters and actions, from different moments and places in the text and in its

[handwritten margin note: i.e. we never really forget "artifice"?]

represented reality, to flow into one another through juxtapositions
—echoes—trapped in the web of pattern. Yet each of these unions,
at its most audacious, gives itself away, betrays the limits of its self-
enclosure, betrays—that is—the mistakenness that licenses the verbal daring that it will not surrender. Such a union may not only
summon up our disapproving awareness of those other texts composed of conventional and less problematic enclosures within which
our culture persuades us to perceive our "normal reality," but—
more importantly—may also lead us to subvert them, helping us
resist their tendency to rest within the realm of difference that turns
them institutional and precludes or represses perceptions viewed as
subversive. But in the vision indulged by the metaphor, the resistance finds an alternative, and indeed a subversive, perception—and
semiotic.

In meaning to extend my treatment of metaphor, as organicism
would empower it, to all these poetic elements—to character and
action and modes of representation as well as language—I have
broadened it into becoming a synecdoche for the literary text itself.
I have done so because I am convinced that it is the duplicitous
relationship—synchronically sustained—between the thrust to
identity and the retreat into difference that distinguishes the poetic
response, and that it is in verbal metaphor that we perceive it most
clearly, though we then can apply our way of reading metaphor
more broadly to other elements in the poem. Hence in my first
chapter I began with the Renaissance lyric, claiming a reading method
that I shall be widening here. It is the temptation to metaphor that
contaminates all that functions as poem for us, contaminates it, and
turns it subversive. That is, on the one side, it subverts our commonsense impulse to read differentially only, by forcing us to see
the blendings of entities that language would normally seek to keep
separate; and, on the other side, it subverts our poetic impulse to
subdue all differences into a oneness, by nudging us into being
aware of the dangerous and repressive limits of such enclosure. This
sense of subversion—subversion both of the institutions established
by the institutional language of difference and of the paradoxical
totalities constructed by the poet's language of identity—returns us

from the linguistic concern with metaphor and its other to the thematic and existential consequences (or causes) of our verbal plight. And recent post-structuralist theory, despite its contrary claims, has only reassured me in my conviction that the thematic consequences of metaphor cannot be evaded and should not, therefore, be ignored.

I am arguing that we may perceive an analogy between the push toward identity that, within the linguistic realm, sets forth the metaphorical in opposition to the differential and the push toward the counter-propositional that, within the thematic realm, sets forth poetic vision as subversive to the rule of propositions and the institutions they foster and help sustain. Indeed, more than an analogy, they may represent two sides of one coin, with the subversive as that which—both thematic and existential—turns propositions self-contradictory, each exposing its own antithesis and turning the moral, as institutional, against itself. Indeed, might we not argue that, far from seeing the organic as closed, it is—as the ground for the literary as metaphoric—the only sort of discursive form that cannot be closed? Instead it is the conventional discursive forms created by the differential realm of language—the forms that we impose so that we may order our experienced and moral worlds—it is these forms that are utterly closed within their demands for a coherence that allows us to keep the world together as we seek to keep ourselves together. This is the closure that serves the pressure to institutionalize these forms into ideology, which then requires us to serve *it,* to the exclusion of all that might undermine it.

These "normal" discursive forms may appear to be simply and unqualifiedly referential as the New Critics—after Richards—too easily insisted out of their contempt for such forms, a contempt born of a desire to privilege metaphor. But post-structuralists—Derrida and Foucault each in his own way—have taught us what a self-deception this was, finding these apparently nonpoetic forms text-ridden or episteme-ridden and thus always already contained in pre-committed verbal figures. These are the closures whose totalizing consequences threaten to subdue us all to their power. But it has been my effort in these essays to argue that, far from working to establish closure, the poetic, conceived organically—that is, within the self-undoing drive toward metaphor—yields a duplicity that can break us free of the prison-house of epistemic language. It provides the model for language's infinitely subversive self-unravelings. And it is the self-doubling metaphoric habit of mind, built into our structures of verbal response through the secular *imitatio Christi* of the late Middle Ages and Renaissance, that allows the poetic structure—in these parodied secular versions—to work upon us still. It breaks free of the hold of institutions by undoing institutional discourse. The poem may reveal, *in extremis,* what it is for language to trap us within its ultimate capacity for self-enclosure, but it also slips the knot that turns the language against itself and gives us an airy escape.

Because I was not attentive in the late 1950s to the linguistic dimensions of what I then was calling "the tragic vision," I concentrated upon its thematic-existential dimensions.[8] I would now claim that the extremity seized upon by my tragic protagonists can also be described as their being stricken by metaphor, so that the literary works in which they function serve as warnings against an unrelieved metaphorical enclosure. At the same time we are exhilarated by the doubling that shows, though at great expense, a life outside the law — seen as a destructively enclosing structure at once verbal and thematic—that enacts the escape that Kafka's Joseph K. desperately sought but could not find. For a protagonist to be stricken by metaphor is for him or her to feel an identity, an identity both ominous and dangerous, with another character from whom the difference, a quite evident difference, is required for self-preservation. More than a return to the mirror-phase, it is to feel one's adult self trapped within a hall of mirrors in which one looks outward and sees only oneself, losing all awareness of distinctions that would permit moral judgment, and hence the moral life—a life of distinction-making—to be pursued. If the tragic existents, as protagonists, are stricken by metaphor, those who chronicle their stories see duplicitously, at once through them and beyond them, and so find themselves indulging both metaphor and counter-metaphor. This is why Marlow must, at the end of *Heart of Darkness,* free himself from his obsessive identification with Kurtz and yet—as a free gesture toward such identification—must lie for Kurtz to his "intended"; or why, at the end of *Lord Jim,* Marlow must liberate himself from his obsessive identification with Jim so that he can make a judgment *for* Jim, though without being trapped by the attractions of Jim's vainglorious, self-inflicted fate. For Marlow in the end resists the dangerous equations leading to the "one-of-us" identity that has gripped many others in the novel, indeed that killed Captain Brierly. And from the start it was Jim who set in motion that fateful, self-implicating sequence of identifications when he accepts as his own, without distinctions, all the ugly acts and motivations of those who leapt to safety, those who betrayed. He falls into such identifications consistently, ending his career by seeing himself even—and most fatally—in the deadly Mr. Brown.

Those characters I saw in *The Tragic Vision* as tragic existents are committed utterly and without resistance to the extremity of metaphoric identity with another whom they came to see as one with themselves. They thus have given up the life-securing moral instinct that would remind them to withdraw from such blurring of persons and meanings, to withdraw into difference. For moral judgment requires the assumption of difference between the judge and the judged. Whatever the similarities ("there but for the grace of God go I"), the claim of difference must not altogether be given up. Like Marlow, who in both *Heart of Darkness* and *Lord Jim* goes a long way toward metaphor but cannot totally abandon his sense of difference, the narrator-captain resists identity with his secret sharer in the story with that title, however close he comes—as close as he comes to destroying the ship (to eliminating *all* distance between ship and shore) for the sake of that identity which is implied by the title. In all these cases the reader, perceiving both the tragic existent and the tragic visionary-narrator, grasps both the metaphor and its denial, both identity and difference.

If Conrad's narrator can finally resist the extremity of metaphor and with it the unmitigatedly tragic, the tragic existent, like Lord Jim, cannot. We can recall Dostoyevsky's self-dooming protagonists: Ivan Karamazov, who persists in finding himself reflected in Smerdyakov, his degraded half-brother, and in sharing with him the guilt of parricide; or Prince Myshkin, the idiot saint whose idiocy consists in his finding himself complicit in the crimes of those morally lost creatures he should be condemning for his own sanity's sake. We may recall also how much of Joseph K.'s anguish in Kafka's *The Trial,* as well as his isolation from his fellows, arises both from his attraction to the condemned as one of them and from the fear that drives others away out of an anxiety that insists on their difference from him in his presumed guilt. Or I could cite Thomas Mann's *Doctor Faustus,* at the outer edge of the border where the modern transforms itself into the postmodern. Adrian Leverkühn, Mann's Faustus, identifies creativity with illness and the ultimate realization of form with the breakthrough to the formless: identifies endless echo with silence. All these dangerous blurrings of oppositions proliferate, while a terrified Serenus Zeitblom seeks to restore distinctions in the modesty of his narration. This may be the ultimate case among these representative modern novels.

Even—or rather especially—in the archetypally tragic case of Hamlet we see the cost of being stricken by metaphor: he for too long allows his revenging hand to be stayed by the potential sameness between the regicide he contemplates performing and the earlier criminal regicide performed by his would-be victim, Claudius, both regicides in part stimulated by a forbidden intention toward the Queen. The threat of such identity between him and Claudius invades his resolve as it invades the dramatic structure of the play, protracts it, and plunges it toward its tragic denouement. But there is also in Hamlet, as there is in *Hamlet,* a countermovement that does recognize the need to see Claudius as an other, so much other that he must be judged and destroyed. So murder competes in Hamlet with murder-as-suicide, difference with identity, distinction between oneself and another with a blurring between them. But of course he waits too long to resolve the two-sided prompting.

It is the metaphor, uncritically indulged, that turns deadly in its obliteration of the differentiating act that would save the fictional

so non clause

character's self from indulging its extremity by allowing it to perform the judgmental act that would preserve it as not altogether *as*
guilty—and so not *as* deserving of destruction—as another, whatever the similarities between the two. The tragic existent, one might
say, has followed the pattern that René Girard might dictate, a
pattern that confounds all distinctions into singleness by means of
the totally mimetic act of doubling that allows one character to be
absorbed within another, accepting thereby the doom of repetition.
In his critical writings Girard, I fear, has himself been so stricken by
metaphor that he remains too blurred by oneness to recover the
balance that would reopen the fiction; by such a reopening the
Girardian critic, threatened with the metaphorical closure that turns
two into one, might have managed at least partly to recover and
reenter the realm of differentness. This attempted recovery is the
retreat from extremity that I chronicled in *The Classic Vision* (1971),
the epilogue to which recites the list of withdrawals and reopenings
that the several chapters were to have traced in a number of
works.

   It seemed to me that one work after another forced upon the
reader (me) the paradoxical sense of metaphor, with its drive to
identity and simultaneity, and metaphor's inexorable other, which
shrewdly and skeptically and—in the end—safely keeps the ever-
separating world of words separated, which sees metaphor as mistake. One can easily multiply the examples of such characters and
their felt equations with others, equations at once total and mistaken. Even in the absence of characters who are themselves stricken
by metaphor, for the reader too there are in most works pairs of
characters (we used to call them "foils") who become versions of
one another, though the differences between them collapse as we
watch. Even as their interests require them to declare such differences as oppositions, we see the text nourishing their growing
interchangeability. We find an extreme model of this collapsing of
polarity in the debates between Settembrini and Naphta in Mann's
The Magic Mountain, in which magisterial rationalism and demon-
iacal irrationalism proceed out of their mutual opposition only to
meet and interchange with one another.

Things went not only by contraries, but also all higgledy-piggledy. The disputants not only contradicted each other, they contradicted themselves. How often had Settembrini not spent his oratory in praise of criticism, as being the aristocratic principle? Yet now it was for its opposite, for "art," that he made the same claim. How often had Naphta not stood for instinct, . . . mere *"factum et fatum,"* before which reason and human pride must never abdicate! But here now was Naphta on the side of the soul and disease, wherein alone true nobility and humanity resided, while Settembrini flung himself into advocacy of nature and her noble sanity, regardless of his inconsistency on the score of emancipation from her. The "Object" and the "Ego" were no less involved in confusion—yes, and here the confusion, moreover, remained constant, was the most literal and incorrigible; so that nobody any longer knew who was the devout and who the free-thinker. . . . Where lay the true position, the true state of man? Should he descend into the all-consuming all-equalizing chaos, that ascetic-libertine state; or should he take his stand on the "Critical-Subjective," where empty bombast and a bourgeois strictness of morals contradicted each other? Ah, the principles and points of view constantly did that; it became so hard for Hans Castorp's civilian responsibility to distinguish between opposed positions, or even to keep the premises apart from each other and clear in his mind, that the temptation grew well-nigh irresistible to plunge head foremost into Naphta's "morally chaotic All."[9]

Shakespeare has of course provided critics with countless possibilities, even extreme ones, of confounding characters who seem opposed, even polar, as—for example—in the rivalry between Antonio and Shylock as to which better deserves to be called *The Merchant of Venice.* I bring up this play in order to return to my differences from René Girard. No one more than Girard has so forcefully used analytic subtlety to turn into a serious and ambiguous question Portia's apparently routine request for identification,

"Which is the merchant here, and which the Jew?" In each such case critical and thematic ingenuity may persuade us to overplay the identity that our shrewdness has uncovered beneath ostensible oppositions. Certainly Girard has been thus persuaded of the interchangeability, indeed the identity, between merchant and merchant, Antonio and Shylock. In accordance with his long-standing critical habit, Girard allows his brilliance of interpretation to lead him to leap uncritically into the totally achieved metaphor, as part of his general theoretical need to proclaim—against Lévi-Strauss—the underlying primacy of undifferentiated ritual over the differentiations of myth, which he takes to be the ground for the structuralist view of language and culture that he rejects. He thus refuses—I think wrongly refuses—to concede that these narrative versions of metaphor must after all function under the jurisdiction of difference that reminds us of the metaphor's insufficiency and of the resilient distinctions between its terms.

It was to help clarify this peculiar doubleness, to deal with such pairings, at once collapsed and differentiated, that I some years ago introduced as my model metaphor (as well as my model *for* metaphor) the "prisoner's dilemma" of game theory in the social sciences. It represents the special pairing that identifies desire with aversion, coupling with polarity, both as the thematic model that relates character to character and as the semiotic model that relates the two terms of a metaphor in their paradoxical search for an identity that only reinforces difference.

The game itself refers to the behavior alternatives of two confederates in crime being separately interrogated by the police, who press each of them in isolation to confess the crime in order to reduce the punishment. Since there is no other incriminating evidence, if both hold out, both are exonerated; but if one confesses and pays the lighter price, the other—on the evidence of the first—is punished fully. Even if both confess, they will suffer something less than the heaviest punishment, though it will not be lightened as much as if the confession of one is instrumental in convicting the other. So there are two choices for each, but four possible outcomes graded by the severity of punishment from none to the most severe, depending on the interaction between the two decisions. The decision of one, by itself, is indecisive.

There is, then, reason for one to take the ultimate chance, to hold out for the best of outcomes, outright release, *depending on* the decision of the other; as there is—under conditions of the usual mutual mistrust—reason to play it safe by "copping a plea": reason, that is, not simply to confess but actually to be the first to confess— to confess without delay. The extreme choice is either the best or the worst, while the compromise choice can proceed only from distrust of the other. It is within these carefully measured gradations that weigh behavior against punishment, within this bewildering array of risks tied to payoffs, of extremities and compromises, severity and security, that the game is played out with its balance of uncertain guesses and not-altogether-foreseeable outcomes. For it is played out for each with the other felt as another self, yet as a reflection of one's own self, though only as a mirror gives us at once ourselves and our reversed selves or ourselves *as* our reversed selves. This is a relationship at once thematic and semiotic.

I see this relationship—both in the prisoner's-dilemma game and in the duplicitous relations between either two fictional characters or the two terms of a poem's metaphor—as one emblematized in the allegorical figure invented by Joan Krieger for my book, *Poetic Presence and Illusion.* As I describe the emblem elsewhere, "In it two identical and opposed mythical creatures, in multiple images, are invariably twinned in their mutual relations: they look, open-eyed, at one another or are turned, eyes closed, away; and they are together too in sharing the blackness of type or the black-enclosed outlines of blank space." [10] The riddle she writes to accompany the figure makes my point as it explicates the title of that book: "This creature fabricated / multiplies itself, but moves not; / sees itself, or sees not; / exists twice, and is not."

So I enlarge upon my semiotic and thematic extrapolations from the prisoner's-dilemma game and adapt it to my own purposes through reference to this emblem. Let me quote from my effort elsewhere to describe the dilemma as an existential dilemma that becomes the model for metaphor.

In the game model, each of two partners in crime, being interrogated separately, is dependent on—but cut off from—the other's testimony. Each must decide either to cooperate with the police by turning against the other out of fear of the other's confession or to remain a faithful confederate in hopes that his partner remains equally true to him. So the choice between plea-bargaining or holding out with a claim of innocence is tied to the interpretation by *either* of the partner's likely choice, which is similarly dependent on a reading of *his*.

Each of the partners, then, must define himself through his speculative interpretation of the other as he moves through a process of at once differentiating his own interest and being forced to identify it with the other's interest. He is both a separate individual and a twin, one that can serve his individuality only by discovering another's precisely like his own. His sense of himself as real is riveted to his illusionary sense of the other, and yet he is aware that in the companion interrogation cell it is all being reversed, that the other turns his back to convert the first criminal into a similar illusion that confounds separateness and identity. Like the creatures in the . . . emblem, they see each other, or see not. Or should I view them as a single, divided creature rather than as two doubly bound creatures and say (as the accompanying riddle does) that it "sees itself, or sees not"? This is just the archetypal duplicity long recorded about what it is to be identical twins, born of one egg. So, projected out of this model, presence can be defined only by its illusionary double, by its own vision of its illusionary other, at once absorbed into the self and rejected as an other.

For the prisoner trapped in his dilemma, in the silence of his isolated cell confronting himself and his mate (confronting himself as his mate), the question of which is the signifier and which the signified in his interpretive problem is one that shifts on him as he ponders it. I press this semiotic doubleness or controlled instability to characterize the relation between the two elements of poetic metaphor, conceived in the broadest sense; or, indeed, to characterize the relation between presence and illusion themselves, which I find similarly twinned. As with the prisoners, or the creatures in the emblem, the signifier and signified—like the tenor and vehicle in metaphor —*both* look at each other in mutual mimesis, and turn away in separateness—though in this act too they remain twinned and mimetic.[11]

In the prisoner's-dilemma model, as in the emblem, we have the representation—at once semiotic and thematic—of the paradoxical pairing that identifies coupling with aversion, twinning with division, the openness of mutual dependence with the closure of autonomy. The literary examples I cited earlier could all be recalled here to enforce these observations. Such a pairing of course achieves its most extreme polarity in relations between male and female, the hermaphroditic trope of two-in-one coupling which is itself coupled with the mutual aversion of duality. We have seen this paradox locked into our linguistic history at least since the Christological language habit that was at the source of my first chapter. The hermaphroditic temptation is asserted and yet undone in the verbal enactment of sexual difference, an act of both rescue and damnation, perhaps the profoundest version of the prisoner's-dilemma model. We can think, for example, of Strindberg's Julie and her counterpart, Jean, with whom she confounds herself while seeking polarity from him. In *Miss Julie* we watch the uneasy succession of merging and splitting—at once of sex and of social class—in the mimetic act of doubling *and* the recognition of doubling as a mistake that once acknowledged, splits itself off in its need to assert differentiation— indeed opposition. Thus the creatures in the figure that look to one another in the claim of becoming one and that turn away in the claim of distinctness, even autonomy. The prisoners, as these creatures, have their fates twinned, their decisions entwined—each seeing the other as himself—even as their self-interest would damn the other to save the self.

Each must say, "I feel the need to assert my desires as separate and opposed to those of my twin-as-enemy. But in so doing I am

repeating and thus becoming my other, on whose self-assertion the
meaning and outcome of my own self-assertion depends. But that
other is at the same time repeating me with actions similarly dependent on mine. Yet there is an escape from such closure: In accepting
this identity of act in our identity of interest, I yet know that *my*
interest, as differentiated, proclaims identity as a mistake and would
damn the other to save myself, even as that other must think the
same. And yet—whatever our self-interest leads each of us to decide
—we act together, as one, in twinned acts whose polarity-in-unison
would bring on mutual destruction." Is there a more telling sum-
mary of the paradoxical relations that move and bring on the doom
in *Miss Julie*? Or a more telling example of how the prisoner's
dilemma, once we return the thematic to the semiotic, can lead us
from metaphor, to metaphor as mistake, to metaphor *and* mistake?

I have been arguing, then, using Girard as *my* foil, that difference
must be seen as remaining after all, even as we are being urged—
via verbal and dramatic duplicity—to see these differences as reflections of one another. Yet metaphor—with the sense of identity,
verbal presence, and verbal closure that it provides—is needed to
kindle our awareness of the complicating blurrings that force us to
recognize the inadequacies of the simplistic act of differentiation
that too often characterizes the self-righteousness of moral judgment
and *its* discourse. Metaphor persuades us to reject a too easy rationalism, and seduces us by its enclosure within its own irrationalism,
within its own attempt to provide an uncanny discourse for the
arbitrary equations of the unconscious. It lends the discursive strength
needed to make intelligible the language of immediacy, of visions,
of dreams, against the trim, at times enslaving, categories of the
daylight language we cannot altogether give up.

So literature, as the principal agent of metaphor, shocks us into
metaphor and, once stricken, it is hard for us to return to the canny
realm of everyday difference, though we do so as wiser creatures.
But return we must, if we are to move beyond (or rather move back
from) the extremity that precludes distinction-making, so that we
may make judgments after all, though these are now softened and
humanized, having been taught to be tentative by the metaphorical

reductions we have witnessed. And it is metaphor itself, in its self-referential capacity to point to its own insufficiency as no more than an aesthetic reduction, that, having lured us within its confinements, encourages us to blink it away and then to look again at the world into which its self-denial opens us.[12] Imprisoned in our own dilemmas, we can now neither blindly hope to maximize the option we decide upon nor decline to make a decision at all. (I realize as I write these words that I have not after all left Hillis Miller's concern with *The Ethics of Reading,* the subject of these Wellek Lectures just two years ago. This common interest, and even perhaps our not so dissimilar objectives, make me feel—despite the large differences between us—less isolated in my efforts in these chapters, though, of course, I hardly mean to suggest collapsing *those* differences into identity.)

I might suggest yet another strange pairing of entities—textual entities—that, in the consciousness of the reader or observer, allows closure to break itself, to break into openness. This pairing provides us with a paradoxical union between what it is beyond the text that the text reflects and the text itself as self-sufficient. It thus confronts us at once with presentation and representation, with the fictional text in itself and the Ur-text that it reminds us of, that seems to lie in wait behind it, that shadows it: what I call the "shadow text." The text's metaphoricity points to itself even as the counter-metaphorical thrust within the metaphor points to that "shadow text" beyond. The shadow text is larger than the text: it is the reflection of the text's metaphors in the differential realm of metonymy, in the inexact and interchangeable land of paraphrase. For the shadow text is also a shadow genre, loose container for the text but not, finally, responsible for it. In its quest for uniqueness, the individual text resists its generic shadow, as the word resists the synonym. Yet in some sense each *is* seen as yielding to what it would resist. Again, as with the prisoners in their dilemma, one must entertain the coexistence of interdependence and autonomy, of openness and closure in theme and in sign relations.

Behind the fictional enclosure we attribute to the literary text, then, is the shadow that is the genre or is the several genres—

literary or generally linguistic or perhaps historical and experiential
—that we cannot help attributing to it, a shadow that is the outside
equivalent, in our imagined "real" world, of the inside fiction we are
exploring. Obviously, the generic shadow that our literary knowledge leads us to impose will vary with the stimulating text and our
conventional sense of its "kind." Behind the make-believe of the
novel or narrative poem lies the presumably more "real" form it is
at once imitating and parodying: such "real" forms as the presumably fact-bound history or biography or, in the case of first-person
narrative, autobiography or journal. Behind the first-person lyric
looms a similar shadow of the confessional, as behind its metaphors
we sense the prosaic paraphrase composed of synonyms performing
metonymically. And, as I suggested toward the end of my second
chapter, the drama in its every moment at once denies and reminds
us of the apparently real "happening" that we both see within it and
see it—since it is but an Aristotelian imitation—as differing *from*.

   In each case the relation between the text and its generic textual
shadow (often seen as the supposedly "realistic" shadow) is a duplicitous one, with the text, as parody, reminding us of the shadowy
textual equivalent that it is *not*. We owe much of the text's intelligi-
bility to the shadow text or genre which we impose upon it, and
which consequently appears to control it. Yet the text struggles to
free itself in its own fictionality which we see as working toward its
self-sufficiency. We find meaning in the text by referring it to its
shadow or shadows, although it seeks to define itself by transforming what the shadow seems to have made available. I am, of course,
speaking of our response rather than of the text itself, so that many
so-called nonliterary texts can be treated in this literary way (many
now term it this "rhetorical" way), thereby enlarging indefinitely the
domain of available texts for such treatment.

   What we read in each of these several kinds of texts is both the
attempt by the shadow text, seen as a universalized shadow genre,
to claim, indeed to subsume, the single text at hand, thus keeping it
generically open, and the attempt by the text itself to make its claim
as a unique play of forces that would seal it off in its own breakaway
freedom. But I have urged that we also find in the text an element

of self-denial that would undo organic self-enclosure and open the work toward its shadow—open the metaphor toward its metonymic shadow—so that the duplicitous character of our response would be sustained without resolution. Nevertheless, in this doubleness the literary text appears to function to subvert the authority of the shadow genre, persuading us to concede that its metonymic shadow can never quite, as metonym, be its equivalent. In effect, within the text the genre is carnivalized, converted into *genera mixta,* its language exploded into a heteroglossia. This process, as my terminological borrowings indicate, is much like that which Bakhtin sees as characterizing the novel in its historical process of discovering itself as anti-genre.

If I may proceed in this Bakhtinian spirit, I suggest that the hegemonic discourse functioning in a culture at a given moment in its history is yet another of the shadow textual genres with which the text struggles and which it appears to subvert, even though the text may also be seen as falling within its control. This enlargement of the notion of shadow texts, as broader discursive genres, gives us an opening from the literary work to social history without precluding the textual power of its own internal play of forces. Indeed, it is only in this play that the text can perform its special subversive function, its combination of reflections and self-reflections that allows it both to represent an authoritarian shadow text and to *mis*represent it by representing it duplicitously. Because of its total dedication to this play, the literary text can function for us as a model for those texts we do not read as literary, discourses that do not at once subvert and self-subvert. It becomes one of the places where the surrounding culture, as represented by its discursive formation, gives itself away by being seen as undercutting itself.

From the first, these chapters have been intended to enlarge our response to the usual charges made against so-called organic theory because it is seen as justifying the conception of literature as a sort of discourse differentiated from others, a specially closed discourse constructed out of deviations from other, more "normal" uses of discourse which are, in comparison, seen as open. But, as I am now presenting literature against its other, I am suggesting the reverse:

that it is the literary work—or what we read as a literary work—
that in its duplicity has an openness unavailable to the more singleminded discursive alternative that would reflect, unchallenged, the
closure of a hegemonic discursive system. It is in this sense that I
have referred to the freedom we can find in the fictional duplicity of
the literary work, in which any totalizing internal system undoes
itself in the very process of seeking closure.[13] By contrast, those
texts (termed nonliterary), which we read as seeking to avoid self-
subversion, seem utterly subservient to the tendency of any one of
either the ruling *or* revolutionary discourses of a culture to impose
itself as a totalizing discourse. Such texts reflect rather than resist
that discourse, thereby leaving to literature alone a disruptive function.

I am pleased to find Edward Said (our next Wellek lecturer)
writing in agreement with this view. In his extraordinarily sensitive
appreciation of the legacy of R. P. Blackmur, Said quotes approv-
ingly Blackmur's prescription for the function of literature: ". . . the
true business of literature, as of all intellect, critical or creative . . . is
to remind the powers that be, simple and corrupt as they are, of the
turbulence they have to control. There is a disorder vital to the
individual which is fatal to society."[14]

Out of my conviction about this function for literature I have,
throughout these essays, tried to get beyond the simplistic attack on
organicism that overlooked its often subliminal commitment to that
dynamism and resistance which directed literature's subversive relation to any of the dominant languages of its culture. Without this
commitment to resist, all that we would have was nonliterature—or
what we read as nonliterature—now remaining as the subservient
agent of totalization. Although writers and their texts can never
escape being historically contingent, in this view the literary work
determines history as much as history determines the literary work.
But of course what is called a literary work is determined by the way
any particular text is read.

What is being suggested about the special authority of the literary
work is in accord with Adorno's statement in defense of the aes-

thetic as a social-political instrument: "The greatness of works of art lies solely in their power to let those things be heard which ideology conceals."[15] That power, Adorno argues, derives from the peculiar capacity of works of art to function "like windowless monads," though only while "representing something which is other than they," a "something" otherwise not representable. So it is the closure itself that ensures a special opening, an opening to the historical, "to the empirical other" by the aesthetic self-enclosure: "Without a heterogeneous moment, art cannot achieve autonomy," but an autonomy "shot through with historical and geographical reporting."[16] This extraordinary, if paradoxical, claim for the literary text as at once aesthetic and anthropological in function is one I have been urging for some time,[17] although I hope I have extended and deepened my arguments in these essays.

I acknowledge the obvious fact that, while—whether they are Adorno's or mine—these are transhistorical claims about how literature can function, they are being made from inside history, so that their vision is obviously affected, and limited, by that fact. In other words, I am aware of the privileged position being assumed by my narrative version of history and my classification of its phenomena, and thus by the claims I am making here. It is a privilege that theorists cannot avoid assuming: it is assumed even by those who would use it to privilege history and history's powers of de-privileging all transhistorical theoretical claims by reducing them to itself. Nevertheless, I want no misunderstanding about my awareness of the limitations of my own historical position and its reflections upon the narrative argument I have projected in these essays. In hoping that, among the claims I have made, there might be a residue worth considering after historical reduction had done its work on me, I am myself attempting to give voice to what is being repressed these days by the hegemony of historical reduction that seeks to govern current theory. Mine hardly presumes to be a literary work, of course, though I still seek in it enough discursive freedom to challenge a new historicist orthodoxy that is, in spite of itself, assuming an increasingly inflexible metaphysic.

Organicism as a metaphor, and in the attitude toward metaphor that it authorizes, has been my fellow prisoner in these chapters as I have been wriggling in my dilemma, seeking to go my way and worrying about how it goes *its*. As I have come to view it, what secures the metaphor also disperses it by letting our skeptical side see its metonymic shadow. From organicism the modernist, as poet or critic, inherits the impulse to collapse all the variations of a motley cultural history into a mythic union—their metaphorical embodiment—except that the union finds within itself the divergent lines moving out from its center into postmodern dispersion. This remarkable coexistence of both the enclosing circle and its lines radiating outward (from its radii) is brilliantly sketched for us in Mann's *Doctor Faustus,* that ultimate modernist novel whose modernism, at its peril, dissolves into its own early and prophetic postmodernism.[18] It at once weaves and unravels—by reference to music and text, parody and subservience, form and anti-form—the resistant threads of Zeitblom's narration of Leverkühn's baffling career and the even more baffling apotheosis of his final work.

> A mammoth variation-piece of lamentation . . . broadens out in circles, each of which draws the other resistlessly after it: movements, large-scale variations, which correspond to the textual units of chapters of a book and in themselves are nothing else than series of variations. But all of them go back for the theme to a highly plastic fundamental figure of notes, which is inspired by a certain passage of the text.[19]

However, in that novel the variations remain as decentered as the twelve-tone scale that plays upon the twelve syllables of that Faustian text ("For I die as a good and as a bad Christian"). And the text itself is to the end indeterminate, with its insistence on the "good" and the "bad" yoked in the "Christian." So on the one hand there seems to be—however unstable—a source, an origin, in the text, for the variations, and yet, on the other hand, the variations seem not to point beyond themselves ("in themselves are nothing else than series of variations"). Here, in sustaining both self-propagating variations and an all-propagating theme that would be their source, Mann one last time represents the paradox latent in the organicist tradition as I have traced it in these essays.

I chose this quotation more than a quarter-century ago as my epigraph to *The Tragic Vision: Variations on a Theme in Literary Interpretation* (1960)—as I cite it again now—in hopes that, like Leverkühn's ultimate work, *The Lamentation of Doctor Faustus* (at least according to Mann's Zeitblom), it could take on a different meaning, as the sound of the symphonic cantata's final notes "changes its meaning" in the silence.

> For listen to the end, listen with me: one group of instruments after another retires, and what remains, as the work fades on the air, is the high G of a cello, the last word, the last fainting sound, slowly dying in a pianissimo-fermata. Then nothing more: silence, and night. But that tone which vibrates in silence, which is no longer there, to which only the spirit hearkens, and which was the voice of mourning, is so no more. It changes its meaning; it abides as a light in the night. (p. 491)

"It would be but a hope beyond hopelessness, the transcendence of despair—not betrayal to her, but the miracle that passes belief." "Pianissimo-fermata": the dying fall, moving into the ultimate closure, the surrounding silence, but only by resounding beyond itself, and thus opening outward.[20]

Zeitblom's paradoxical discussion of Leverkühn's theme and variations (which is also and at the same time *his* variations that yet become his de-thematizing theme) serves as *my* shadow text here in order to help my own lamentation, on behalf of the fate of organicism, to change *its* meaning, or even to find its meaning, here at the end, with this quotation, which functions as my conclusion, my final notes. In a literary work, as in my argument, the theme may be seen as dissipating into both a series of concentric circles and endless linear extensions of text, nothing but variations—on what?—after all. And the unrepresentable is back to haunt us all, though we at least can feel we approach it in the opacity of the literary works that surround it, and yet let it escape for us to follow. Those final sounds are what we must carry with us, into the silence, beyond the last note.

NOTES

1. *Anatomy of Criticism* (Princeton: Princeton University Press, 1957), pp. 115–28. The quotations appear on pp. 117 and 124.
2. *Anatomy of Criticism,* pp. 63–65.
3. See the opening paragraphs of Arnold's "The Study of Poetry" (1880), Richards' early testament, *Science and Poetry* (1926), and my essay that relates the two and ties them to Eliot as well: "The Critical Legacy of Matthew Arnold; or, The Strange Brotherhood of T. S. Eliot, I. A. Richards, and Northrop Frye," *Poetic Presence and Illusion: Essays in Critical History and Theory* (Baltimore: Johns Hopkins University Press, 1979), pp. 92–107.
4. *Burnt Norton,* Section V.
5. See my *"Murder in the Cathedral:* The Limits of Drama and the Freedom of Vision," *The Classic Vision: The Retreat from Extremity* (Baltimore: Johns Hopkins University Press, 1971), pp. 337–62.
6. A recent formulation of this argument appears in " 'A Waking Dream': The Symbolic Alternative to Allegory," *Words About Words About Words: Theory, Criticism, and the Literary Text* (Baltimore: Johns Hopkins University Press, 1988), pp. 271–88.
7. This is what my book *The Classic Vision* seeks at length to argue. See the diagrams and explication on pp. 24–27.
8. But note my one try at turning the vision linguistic:

> . . . under the pressure and shock of an extreme situation, protagonists like those we have been observing are forced to reject forever the intellectual and human comforts of the "ethical," the deceptively rational life. For writers who deal in extremity, where characters are suddenly and utterly confronted by absurdity, the existential paradoxes are seen to be unresolvable as they point to the inadequacy of any systematically moral disposition. In viewing existential reality as extra-ethical in this sense, I am again reasserting in thematic terms the aesthetic claim that the poetic mode of discourse is extra-propositional. The propositional, then, becomes the discursive equivalent of that "ethical" substitute for existence, moral philosophy; and the poetic, contextually defined, becomes the discursive equivalent of that existential realization into which the extreme situation propels its victim (*The Tragic Vision* [New York: Holt, Rinehart and Winston, 1960], p. 246).

9. *The Magic Mountain,* trans. H. T. Lowe-Porter (New York: Alfred A. Knopf, Inc., 1951), pp. 466–68.

10. *Words About Words,* pp. 195–96.

11. *Ibid.,* pp. 196–97.

12. See the "Epilogue" to *The Classic Vision,* pp. 365–67, in which I summarize, in each of the works treated in that book, both the metaphorical reductions and the breaking free of them.

13. I remind the reader of the enlargement of this category by those who find ways to read many "nonliterary" texts in accordance with these methods, thus denying *their* monolithic character as well. I would suggest that this tactic only reinforces my claim about the role played by literature in leading us toward such readings.

14. Edward Said, "The Horizon of R. P. Blackmur," *Raritan* (Fall 1986), 6: 37.

15. Theodor Adorno, "Lyric Poetry and Society," *Telos* (Summer 1974) 20: 58.

16. Adorno, *Aesthetic Theory,* trans. C. Lenhardt (London: Routledge & Kegan Paul, 1984), pp. 7, 9. See also the section on "The work of art as a monad: immanent analysis," pp. 257–60: ". . . art works are hermetically closed off and blind, yet able in their isolation to represent the outside world" (p. 257).

17. See especially chapter 7 ("The Aesthetic as the Anthropological: The Breath of the Word and the Weight of the World"), *Theory of Criticism: A Tradition and Its System* (Johns Hopkins University Press, 1976), pp. 179–206. There is a much earlier claim for poetic discourse as both closed and open, as at once mirror and window, in *A Window to Criticism: Shakespeare's Sonnets and Modern Poetics* (Princeton: Princeton University Press, 1964), pp. 33–37. There, by way of the opposing diagrams and positions of I. A. Richards and Max Eastman— one representing the relation between language and the world (a correspondence theory) and the other representing the relation of language to its own internal-izing system (a coherence theory)—I seek to join their objectives as appropriate, if paradoxical, objectives for poetry.

18. In a similar, if not analogous, way I hope in these chapters to have demonstrated how some modernist (as late organicist) criticism—like mine, I confess—seeks through itself, yet by itself, to become a prophetic postmodernist criticism.

19. *Doctor Faustus,* trans. H. T. Lowe-Porter (New York: Alfred A. Knopf, 1948), p. 487.

20. Herbert Lehnert reminds me to mention that, although the *Lamentation* is a posthumous work, these are not Zeitblom's final words. Instead, this analytic and allegorical description of the cantata, with its crucial speculation about its final notes, occurs in the text well before the narration of Leverkühn's death, or his final words—or even his lapsing into inarticulateness. Indeed, it occurs well before Adrian's striking of the dissonant chord that is all of the *Lamentation* that is played in his lifetime, or in the course of the novel. This placement of Zeitblom's discussion of the closing notes of the *Lamentation* allows his words (like the final note) to echo—in the very text—beyond themselves, although later words seem to deny, or override, them. (The one "strongly dissonant chord" struck by Adrian, accompanied by the "wail which will ring forever" in Zeitblom's ears, may well be the ironically pessimistic counterpart to that hope-

fully resonant high G of the cello with which, we were told earlier, the *Lamentation* leaves us.) And yet these words on the *Lamentation* do remain with most readers as the last words after all—and in spite of what follows them. Mann encourages their echoing power by invoking them at the end of the novel in Zeitblom's closing prayer for Germany's future: "When will she [Germany] reach the bottom of the abyss? When, out of uttermost hopelessness—a miracle beyond the power of belief—will the light of hope dawn?"

I am of course aware of Adorno's role in persuading Mann to alter and complicate the degree of closure and of openness—of hopelessness and of hope, death and transfiguration—in those crucial final words of Zeitblom's description. Is it not, then, especially fitting that Adorno's words have figured so importantly for me in these chapters?

A CHECKLIST
OF WRITINGS
BY AND ABOUT
MURRAY KRIEGER
A SELECTED BIBLIOGRAPHY

Compiled by Eddie Yeghiayan

Writings by Murray Krieger

1949

Review of Charles Tennyson's *Alfred Tennyson*. *Christian Science Monitor* (June 30, 1949):11.

Review of David Dortort's *The Post of Honor*. *Christian Science Monitor* (May 13, 1949):20.

Review of Jean Bloch-Michel's *The Witness*. *Christian Science Monitor* (October 6, 1949):15.

Review of Ramón José Sender's *The Sphere*. *Christian Science Monitor* (May 24, 1949):18.

Review of Walter Van Tilburg Clark's *The Track of the Cat*. *Christian Science Monitor*, (June 11, 1949):22.

1950

"Creative Criticism: A Broader View of Symbolism." *Sewanee Review* (Winter 1950), 58(1):36–51.

"The Unliterary Criticism of Determinism." Review of Alex Comfort's *The Novel and Our Time*. *Western Review* (Summer 1950), 14(4):311–314.

1951

"*Measure for Measure* and Elizabethan Comedy." *PMLA* (June 1951), 66(4):775–784.

1952

"Critics at Work." Review of John Crowe Ransom, ed., *The Kenyon Critics*. *Western Review* (Summer 1952), 16(4):325–328.
"Toward a Contemporary Apology for Poetry." Ph. D. Dissertation, Ohio State University, 1952.
    See abstract in *Dissertation Abstracts* (June 1958), 18(6):2142–2144.

1953

"The Ambiguous Anti-Romanticism of T. E. Hulme." *ELH* (March 1953), 20(1):300–314.
Edited (with Eliseo Vivas.) *The Problems of Aesthetics: A Book of Readings*. New York: Rinehart, 1953.

1955

"Benedetto Croce and the Recent Poetics of Organicism." *Comparative Literature* (Summer 1955), 7(3):252–258.

1956

"*Dover Beach* and the Tragic Sense of Eternal Recurrence." *University of Kansas City Review* (Autumn 1956), 23(1):73–79.
The New Apologists for Poetry. Minneapolis: University of Minnesota Press, 1956; London: Oxford University Press, 1956.
    Contents:
    Preface: vii-x
    Introductory:3–28.
    Section I The Creative Process: Science, Poetry, and the Imagination: 30–110.
        1 T. E. Hulme: Classicism and the Imagination:31–45.
        2 T. S. Eliot: Expression and Impersonality:46–56.
        3 I. A. Richards: Neurological and Poetic Organization:57–63.
        4 The Requirements of an Organic Theory of Poetic Creation:64–76.
        5 The Organic Theory: Support and Defection:77–89.
        6 The Uniqueness of the Poetic Imagination:90–110.
    Section II The Aesthetic Object: Science, Poetry, and Language:111–163.
        7 I. A. Richards: Some Tools for an Organic Criticism:113–122.
        8 The Transformation of Richards: A Contextual Theory of the Aesthetic Object:123–139.
        9 The Contextual Theory: Further Qualifications and Counter-Qualifications:140–155.
        10 A Note on the Objectivity of Value:156–163.

Section III The Function of Poetry: Science, Poetry, and Cognition:165–201.
11 Some Older Theories about Poetry and Truth:167–181.
12 Some Conditions for an Apology:182–201.

1957

"Critical Theory, History and Sensibility." Review of René Wellek's *The History of Criticism, 1750–1950, Vol. 1, The Later Eighteenth Century; Vol. 2, The Romantic Age. Western Review* (Winter 1957), 21(2):153–159.
Review of Robert M. Browne's *Theories of Convention in Contemporary American Criticism. MLN* (November 1957), 72(7):551–553.

1958

"Critical Dogma and the New Critical Historians." Review of William K. Wimsatt's and Cleanth Brooks' *Literary Criticism. Sewanee Review* (January–March 1958), 66(1):161–177.
"Tragedy and the Tragic Vision." *Kenyon Review* (Spring 1958), 20(2):281–299.

1959

"Conrad's *Youth:* A Naive Opening to Art and Life." *College English* (March 1959), 20(6):275–280.
"The Dark Generations of *Richard III." Criticism* (Winter 1959), 1(1):32–48.

1960

"Recent Criticism, 'Thematics,' and the Existential Dilemma." *Centennial Review of Arts and Science* (Winter 1960), 4(1):32–50.
    A condensed version of the final chapter of *The Tragic Vision: Variations on a Theme in Literary Interpretation* (1960).
The Tragic Vision: Variations on a Theme in Literary Interpretation. New York: Holt, Rinehart and Winston, 1960.
Contents:
    Preface:xix–xxiv.
    1 Tragedy and the Tragic Vision:1–21.
    2 Rebellion and the "State of Dialogue":22–49.
        1 The Huguenot Anti-Ethic of André Gide:22–37.
        2 The State of Monologue in D. H. Lawrence:37–49.
    3 Satanism, Sainthood, and the Revolution:50–85.
        1 André Malraux: Rebellion and the Realization of Self:50–72.
        2 Ignazio Silone: The Failure of the Secular Christ:72–85.
    4 Disease and Health: The Tragic and the Human Realms of Thomas Mann:86–113.
        1 The End of Faustus: Death and Transfiguration:87–102.
        2 *The Magic Mountain:* The Failure of *"Spirituel"* Mediation:102–113.
    5 The World of Law as Pasteboard Mask:114–153.
        1 Franz Kafka: Nonentity and the Tragic:114–144.
        2 Albert Camus: Beyond Nonentity and the Rejection of the Tragic:144–153.

    6 Joseph Conrad: Action, Inaction, and Extremity:154–194.
      1 The Varieties of Extremity:154–179: (*Heart of Darkness:*154–165; *Lord
        Jim:*165–179).
      2 *Victory:* Pseudo Tragedy and the Failure of Vision:179–194.
    7 The Perils of "Enthusiast" Virtue:195–227.
      1 Melville's "Enthusiast": The Perversion of Innocence:195–209.
      2 Dostoevsky's *Idiot:* The Curse of Saintliness: 209–227.
    8 Recent Criticism, "Thematics," and the Existentialist Dilemma:228–268.
      1 Recent Criticism: Formalism and Beyond:229–241.
      2 "Thematics": A Manichaean Consequence:241–257.
      3 A Pseudo-Christian Consequence and the Retreat from Extremity:257–268.

    1961

"Afterword." In Joseph Conrad's *Lord Jim,* pp. 309–317. New York: New American
    Library (Signet Classic edition), 1961.
"Afterword." In Nathaniel Hawthorne's *The Marble Faun; or, The Romance of Monte
    Beni,* pp. 335–346. New York: New American Library, (Signet Classic edition),
    1961.
"Contemporary Literary Criticism: Opening Remarks," and "General Discussion on
    Contemporary Literary Criticism." In Hazard Adams, Bernard Duffey, et al.,
    eds., *Approaches to the Study of Twentieth-Century Literature,* pp. 107–113, 114–
    122. Proceedings of the Conference on the Study of Twentieth-Century Litera-
    ture, First Session, May 2–4, 1961, held at Michigan State University. East
    Lansing: Michigan State University Press, 1961.
"The 'Frail China Jar' and the Rude Hand of Chaos." *Centennial Review of Arts and
    Science* (Spring 1961), 5(2):176–194.
Review of E. M. W. Tillyard's *The Epic Strain in the English Novel. JEGP* (April
    1961), 60(2):311–314.
Review of Robert Boies Sharpe's *Irony in the Drama: An Essay on Impersonation,
    Shock and Catharsis. JEGP* (July 1961), 60(3):550–552.

    1962

"After the New Criticism." *Massachusetts Review* (Autumn 1962), 4(1):183–205.
"Contextualism Was Ambitious." *Journal of Aesthetics and Art Criticism* (Fall 1962),
    21(1):81–88.
"Conrad's *Youth:* A Naive Opening to Art and Life." In Lee Steinmetz, ed., *Analyz-
    ing Literary Works: A Guide for College Students,* pp. 106–112. Evanston, Ill.:
    Row, Peterson, 1962.
    See "Conrad's *Youth:* A Naive Opening to Art and Life" (1959).
"Dostoevsky's *Idiot:* The Curse of Saintliness." In Rene Wellek, ed., *Dostoevsky: A
    Collection of Critical Essays,* pp. 39–52. Englewood Cliffs, NJ: Prentice-Hall, 1962.
    See *The Tragic Vision: Variations on a Theme in Literary Interpretation* (1960),
    chapter 7, #2:209–227.
Review of Joseph Warren Beach's *Obsessive Images; Symbolism in Poetry of the 1930's
    and 1940's. JEGP* (April 1962), 61(2):448–451.

Review of Richard Foster's *The New Romantics: A Reappraisal of New Criticism.* *Criticism* (Fall 1962), 4(4):369–372.

1963

"Every Critic His Own Platonist." *CEA Chap Book* [Supplement to the *CEA Critic* (December 1963), 26(3)]:25–28.

The New Apologists for Poetry. Bloomington: Indiana University Press, Midland Book, 1963.

A paperback reprint of the edition published by the University of Minnesota Press in 1956. Includes a new preface.

"Tragedy and the Tragic Vision." In Laurence Anthony Michel and Richard Benson Sewall, eds., *Tragedy: Modern Essays in Criticism,* pp. 130–146. Englewood, N.J.: Prentice-Hall, 1963.

See "Tragedy and the Tragic Vision" (1958), and *The Tragic Vision: Variations on a Theme in Literary Interpretation* (1960), Chapter 1:1–21.

1964

"Critical Historicism: The Poetic Context and the Existential Context." In Leon Edel, ed., *Literary History and Literary Criticism,* pp. 280–282. Acta of the 9th Congress of the International Federation for Modern Languages & Literatures [FILLM], August 25–31, 1963, held at New York University. New York: New York University, 1964.

"The Poet and His Work—and the Role of Criticism." *College English* (March 1964), 25(6):405–412.

A Window to Criticism: Shakespeare's 'Sonnets' and Modern Poetics. Princeton: Princeton University Press; London: Oxford University Press, 1964.

Contents:

Preface:vii–ix.

Part I The Mirror as Window in Recent Literary Theory:1–70.

  1 The Resort to "Miracle" in Recent Poetics:3–27.

  2 Contextualism and Its Alternatives:28–70.

Part II The Mirror as Window in Shakespeare's *Sonnets:*72–190.

Introductory:73–79.

  1 The Mirror of Narcissus and the Magical Mirror of Love:80–117.

  2 Truth vs. Troth: The Worms of the Vile, Wise World:118–139.

  3 State, Property, and the Politics of Reason:140–164.

  4 The Miracle of Love's Eschatology and Incarnation: 165–190.

Part III The Power of Poetic Effigy:191–218.

The Power of Poetic Effigy:191–218.

1965

"Belief, Problem of," and "Meaning, Problem of." In Alex Preminger, ed., *Encyclopedia of Poetry and Poetics,* pp. 74–76, and 475–479. Princeton, N.J.: Princeton University Press, 1965.

"Contextualism and the Relegation of Rhetoric." In Donald Cross Bryant, ed., *Papers in Rhetoric and Poetic*, pp. 46–58. Conference on Rhetoric and Poetic, November 12–13, 1964, held at the University of Iowa. Iowa City: University of Iowa Press, 1965.

"The Discipline of Literary Criticism." In John C. Gerber, ed., *The College Teaching of English*, pp. 178–197. New York: Appleton-Century-Crofts, 1965.

"Tragedy and the Tragic Vision." In Robert W. Corrigan, ed., *Tragedy: Vision and Form*, pp. 19–33. San Francisco: Chandler, 1965.

   See "Tragedy and the Tragic Vision" (1958), and *The Tragic Vision: Variations on a Theme in Literary Intrepretation* (1960), Chapter 1:1–21.

1966

"Critical Historicism: The Poetic Context and the Existential Context." *Orbis Litterarum* (1966), 21(1):49–60.

   A revised and expanded version of a paper delivered at the 9th Congress of FILLM at New York University in August 1963.

   See "Critical Historicism: The Poetic Context and the Existential Context" (1964).

"The Existential Basis of Contextual Criticism." *Criticism* (Fall 1966), 8(4):305–317.

"*Measure for Measure* and Elizabethan Comedy." In Rolf Soellner and Samuel Bertsche, ed., *Measure for Measure: Text, Source, and Criticism*, pp. 91–99. Boston: Houghton Mifflin, 1966.

   See "*Measure for Measure* and Elizabethan Comedy" (1951).

Edited. *Northrop Frye in Modern Criticism*. Selected papers from the English Institute, September 7–10, 1965. New York and London: Columbia University Press, 1966.

   Includes a foreword:v–viii, and an introductory essay by Murray Krieger, "Northrop Frye and Contemporary Criticism: Ariel and the Spirit of Gravity":1–26

"Tragedy and the Tragic Vision." *Midway* (Summer 1966), 27:2–25.

   See "Tragedy and the Tragic Vision" (1958), and *The Tragic Vision: Variations on a Theme in Literary Interpretation* (1960), Chapter 1:1–21.

The Tragic Vision: Variations on a Theme in Literary Intrepretation. Chicago, and London: University of Chicago Press, Phoenix Books, 1966.

   A paperback reprint of the edition published in New York by Holt, Rinehart and Winston in 1960.

1967

"*Ekphrasis* and the Still Movement of Poetry; or, *Laokoön* Revisited." In Frederick P. W. McDowell, ed., *The Poet as Critic*, pp. 3–26. Conference on the Poet as Critic, October 28–30, 1965, held at the Iowa Center for Modern Letters, University of Iowa. Evanston, Ill: Northwestern University Press, 1967.

The Play and Place of Criticism. Baltimore: Johns Hopkins Press; London: Oxford University Press, 1967.

   Contents:
   Preface:vii–ix.

1 The Play and Place of Criticism:3–16. [See "The Poet and His Work—and the Role of Criticism" (1964).]

I *The Play of Criticism:* 17–128.

2 The Innocent Insinuations of Wit: The Strategy of Language in Shakespear's *Sonnets:* 19–36.

3 The Dark Generations of *Richard III:* 37–52. [See "The Dark Generations of *Richard III*" (1959).]

4 The "Frail China Jar" and the Rude Hand of Chaos:53–68. [See "The 'Frail China Jar' and the Rude Hand of Chaos" (1961).]

5 *Dover Beach* and the Tragic Sense of Eternal Recurrence:69–77. [See "*Dover Beach* and the Tragic Sense of Eternal Recurrence" (1956).]

6 *The Marble Faun* and the International Theme:79–90. [See "Afterword" (1961).]

7 From *Youth* to *Lord Jim:* The Formal-Thematic Use of Marlow:91–104. [See "Conrad's *Youth:* A Naive Opening to Art and Life" (1959), and "Afterword" (1961).]

8 The Ekphrastic Principle and the Still Movement of Poetry; or, *Laokoön* Revisited:105–128. [See "*Ekphrasis* and the Still Movement of Poetry; or, *Laokoön* Revisited" (1967).]

II *The Place of Criticism:* 129–251.

9 The Disciplines of Literary Criticism:131–148. [See "The Discipline of Literary Criticism" (1965).]

10 Joseph Warren Beach's Modest Appraisal:149–152. [See "Review of Joseph Warren Beach's *Obsessive Images: Symbolism in Poetry of the 1930's and 1940's*" (1962).]

11 Contextualism Was Ambitious:153–164. [See "Contextualism Was Ambitious" (1962).]

12 Contextualism and the Relegation of Rhetoric:165–176. (1965).]

13 Critical Dogma and the New Critical Historians:177–193. [See "Critical Dogma and the New Critical Historians" (1958).]

14 Platonism, Manichaeism, and the Resolution of Tension: A Dialogue:195–218. [See "Every Critic His Own Platonist" (1963).]

15 Northrop Frye and Contemporary Criticism: Ariel and the Spirit of Gravity:221–237. [See *Northrop Frye in Modern Criticism* (1966).]

16 The Existential Basis of Contextual Criticism:239–251. [See "The Existential Basis of Contextual Criticism" (1966).]

A volume of collected essays reprinted—occasionally in original form, sometimes slightly revised, sometimes considerably rewritten or supplemented. The essay "The Innocent Insinuations of Wit: The Strategy of Language in Shakespeare's *Sonnets,*" pp. 19–36, appears here for the first time.

1968

"*Bleak House* and *The Trial.*" In Jacob Korg, ed., *Twentieth Century Interpretations of Bleak House: A Collection of Critical Essays,* pp. 103–105. Englewood Cliffs, N.J.: Prentice-Hall, 1968.

See *The Tragic Vision: Variations on a Theme in Literary Interpretation* (1960), chapter 5, #1:138–140.

"Conrad's *Youth:* A Naive Opening to Art and Life." In Michael Timko and Clinton F. Oliver, eds., *38 Short Stories: An Introductory Anthology,* pp. 49–57. New York: Knopf, 1968.

See "Conrad's *Youth:* A Naive Opening to Art and Life" (1959).

"The Continuing Need for Criticism." *Concerning Poetry* (Spring 1968), 1(1):7–21.

"*Ekphrasis* and the Still Movement of Poetry; or, *Laokoön* Revisited." In James Calderwood and Harold E. Toliver, eds., *Perspectives on Poetry,* pp. 323–348. New York: Oxford University Press, 1968.

See "*Ekphrasis* and the Still Movement of Poetry; or *Laokoön* Revisited" (1967), and *The Play and Place of Criticism* (1967), chapter 8:105–128.

"The 'Frail China Jar' and the Rude Hand of Chaos." In Maynard Mack, ed., *Essential Articles for the Study of Alexander Pope,* pp. 301–319. Revised and enlarged edition. Hamden, Conn.: Archon Books; London: Macmillan, 1968.

See " 'The Frail China Jar' and the Rude Hand of Chaos" (1961), and *The Play and Place of Criticism* (1967), chapter 4:53–68.

"Jacopo Mazzoni, Repository of Divine Critical Traditions or Source of a New One?" In Rosario P. Armato and John M. Spalek, eds., *Medieval Epic to the "Epic Theater" of Brecht: Essays in Comparative Literature,* pp. 97–107. 1st Comparative Literature Conference, July 6–7, 1967, held at the University of Southern California. Los Angeles, CA: University of Southern California Press, 1968.

"Literary Analysis and Evaluation—and the Ambidextrous Critic." *Contemporary Literature* (Summer 1968), 9(3):290–310.

Revised version of this essay appears in L. S. Dembo, ed., *Criticism: Speculative and Analytical Essays,* pp. 16–36. Madison, WI: University of Wisconsin Press, 1968.

"The Varieties of Extremity: *Lord Jim.*" In Norman Sherry and Thomas C. Moser, ed., *"Lord Jim": An Authoritative Text,* pp. 437–447. New York: Norton, 1968.

1969

"The Critical Legacy of Matthew Arnold; or, the Strange Brotherhood of T. S. Eliot, I. A. Richards, and Northrop Frye." *Southern Review* (N.S.) (Spring 1969), 5(2):457–474.

"*Eloisa to Abelard:* The Escape from Body or the Embrace of Body." *Eighteenth-Century Studies* (Fall 1969), 3(1):28–47.

"Mediation, Language, and Vision in the Reading of Literature." In Charles S. Singleton, ed., *Interpretation: Theory and Practice,* pp. 211–242. Baltimore: Johns Hopkins Press, 1969.

1970

(With Allen Tate.) "American Criticism, Recent." In Joseph T. Shipley, ed., *Dictionary of World Literary Terms,* pp. 371–374. Revised and enlarged edition. Boston: Writer, 1970.

"The Dark Generations of *Richard III.*" In Melvyn D. Faber, ed., *The Design Within: Psychoanalytic Approaches to Shakespeare*, pp. 347–366. New York: Science House, 1970.

    See "The Dark Generations of *Richard III*" (1959), and *The Play and Place of Criticism* (1967), chapter 3:37–52.

"*Dover Beach* and the Tragic Sense of Eternal Recurrence." In Jonathan Middlebrook, ed., *Matthew Arnold: "Dover Beach,"* pp. 15–23. Columbus, Ohio: Merril, 1970.

    See "*Dover Beach* and the Tragic Sense of Eternal Recurrence" (1956), and *The Play and Place of Criticism* (1967), chapter 5:69–77.

"The 'Frail China Jar' and the Rude Hand of Chaos." In John Dixon Hunt, ed., *Pope: "The Rape of the Lock," A Casebook*, pp. 201–219. Nashville, Tenn.: Aurora, 1970.

    See " 'The Frail China Jar' and the Rude Hand of Chaos" (1961), and *The Play and Place of Criticism* (1967), chapter 4:53–68.

"The Innocent Insinuations of Wit: The Strategy of Language in Shakespeare's *Sonnets.*" In James L. Calderwood and Harold E. Toliver, eds., *Essays in Shakespearean Criticism*, pp. 101–117. Englewood Cliffs, N.J.: Prentice-Hall, 1970.

    See *The Play and Place of Criticism* (1967), chapter 2:19–36.

"The Meaning of Ishmael's Survival." In Herschel Parker and Harrison Hayford, eds., *Moby-Dick as Doubloon: Essays and Extracts, 1851–1970*, pp. 270–271. New York: Norton, 1970.

"*Measure for Measure* and Elizabethan Comedy." In George L. Geckle, ed., *Twentieth Century Interpretations of Measure for Measure: A Collection of Critical Essays*, pp. 104–106. Englewood Cliffs, N.J.: Prentice-Hall, 1970.

    See "*Measure for Measure* and Elizabethan Comedy" (1951).

"*Murder in the Cathedral:* The Limits of Drama and the Freedom of Vision." In Melvin J. Friedman and John B. Vickery, eds., *The Shaken Realist: Essays in Modern Literature in Honor of Frederick J. Hoffman*, pp. 72–79. Baton Rouge: Louisiana State University Press, 1970.

"The State and Future of Criticism: The Continuing Need for Criticism." In Brom Weber, ed., *Sense and Sensibility in Twentieth-Century Writing: A Gathering in Memory of William Van O'Connor*, pp. 1–15. Carbondale and Edwardsville: Southern Illinois University Press; London: Feffer & Simons, 1970.

    Revised version of "The Continuing Need for Criticism" (1968).

1971

The Classic Vision: The Retreat from Extremity in Modern Literature. Baltimore and London: Johns Hopkins Press, 1971.

    Contents:

      Preface:ix–xiv.

      Introduction:1–80

          1 Theoretical: The Tragic Vision and the Classic Vision:3–52. [See "Mediation, Language, and Vision in the Reading of Literature" (1969).]

2 Historical: The "Drab" Vision of Earthly Love:53–80. [See "The Continuing Need for Criticism" (1968).]

Part I The Retreat from Extremity Through the Worship of Bloodless Abstrac-
tions:81–145

   3 "Eloisa to Abelard": The Escape from Body or the Embrace of Body:83–
103. [See *Eloisa to Abelard:* The Escape from Body or the Embrace of
Body" (1969).]

   4 The Cosmetic Cosmos of The Rape of the Lock:105–124

   5 Samuel Johnson: The "Extensive View" of Mankind and the Cost of
Acceptance:125–145.

Part II The Retreat from Extremity Through the Embrace of the Natural
Human Community:147–252

   6 William Wordsworth and the *Felix Culpa:*149–195.

   7 *Adam Bede* and the Cushioned Fall: The Extenuation of Extremity:197–
220.

   8 Postscript: The Naive Classic and the Merely Comic:221–252.

Part III The Retreat from Extremity Through the Acceptance of the Human
Barnyard:253–309

   9 The Human Inadequacy of Gulliver, Strephon, and Walter Shandy—and
the Barnyard Alternative:255–285.

  10 The Assumption of the "Burden" of History in *All the King's Men:*287–
309.

Part IV The Retreat from Extremity Through an Alternative to Sainthood:311–
362

  11 The Light-ening of the "Burden" of History: *Light in August:*313–336.

  12 *Murder in the Cathedral:* The Limits of Drama and the Freedom of
Vision:337–362. [See *Murder in the Cathedral:* The Limits of Drama and
the Freedom of Vision" (1970).]

Epilogue:365–367.

"The Existential Basis of Contextual Criticism." In Hazard Adams, ed., *Critical
Theory Since Plato,* pp. 1224–1231. New York: Harcourt Brace Jovanovich,
1971.

   See "The Existential Basis of Contextual Criticism" (1966), and *The Play and
Place of Criticism* (1967), chapter 16:239–251.

"Fiction, Nature, and Literary Kinds in Johnson's Criticism of Shakespeare." *Eighteenth-Century Studies* (Winter 1971), 4(2):184–198.

"Mediation, Language, and Vision in the Reading of Literature." In Hazard Adams,
ed., *Critical Theory Since Plato,* pp. 1231–1249. New York: Harcourt Brace
Jovanovich, 1971.

   See "Mediation, Language, and Vision in the Reading of Literature" (1969).

"Reply to Robert Kalmey." *Eighteenth-Century Studies* (Winter 1971–1972), 5(2):318–
320.

Reply to Robert Kalmey's "Rhetoric, Language, and Structure in *Eloisa to Abelard,*"
Eighteenth-Century Studies (Winter 1971–1972), 5(2):315–318, which com-

ments on Murray Krieger's *"Eloisa to Abelard:* The Escape from Body or the Embrace of Body" (1969).

"Tragedy and the Tragic Vision." In Robert W. Corrigan, ed., *Tragedy: A Critical Anthology,* pp. 762–775. New York: Houghton Mifflin, 1971.

See "Tragedy and the Tragic Vision" (1958), and *The Tragic Vision: Variations on a Theme in Literary Interpretation* (1960), chapter 1:1–21.

"Die Tragödie und die Tragische Sehweise." In Volkmar Sander, ed., *Tragik und Tragödie,* pp. 279–302. Darmstadt: Wissenschaftliche Buchgesellschaft, 1971.

German translation by Josefa Nünning of "Tragedy and the Tragic Vision" (1958).

1972

Review of Monroe C. Beardsley's *The Possibility of Criticism. English Language Notes* (September 1972), 10(1):75–77.

1973

"The Critic as Person and Persona." In Joseph P. Strelka, ed., *The Personality of the Critic,* pp. 70–92. *Yearbook of Comparative Criticism,* 3. University: Pennsylvania State University Press, 1973.

"Dover Beach and the Tragic Sense of Eternal Recurrence." In Jacqueline E. M. Latham, ed., *Critics on Matthew Arnold: Readings in Literary Criticism,* pp. 40–47. London: George Allen and Unwin, 1973.

See *"Dover Beach* and the Tragic Sense of Eternal Recurrence" (1956), and *The Play and Place of Criticism* (1967), chapter 5: 69–77.

"Introduction." In *The Editor as Critic and the Critic as Editor,* pp. iii–vi. Papers read by J. Max Patrick and Alan Roper at a Clark Library Seminar, November 13, 1971. Los Angeles: William Andrews Clark Memorial Library, UCLA, 1973.

"Mediation, Language, and Vision in the Reading of Literature." In Gregory T. Polletta, ed., *Issues in Contemporary Literary Criticism,* pp. 585–613. Boston: Little, Brown, 1973.

See "Mediation, Language, and Vision in the Reading of Literature" (1969).

Visions of Extremity in Modern Literature. Vol. 1, The Tragic Vision: The Confrontation of Extremity; Vol. 2, The Classic Vision: The Retreat from Extremity. Baltimore and London: Johns Hopkins University Press, 1973.

Paperback reprints of *The Tragic Vision: Variations on a Theme in Literary Interpretation* published in New York by Holt, Rinehart and Winston in 1960, and *The Classic Vision: The Retreat from Extremity in Modern Literature* published in Baltimore and London by the Johns Hopkins Press in 1971.

Includes a new Introduction (in Vol. 1, pp. vii–xvi) entitled "Preface to Visions of Extremity in Modern Literature."

1974

"Contextualism." In Alex Preminger, ed., *Princeton Encyclopedia of Poetry and Poetics,* pp. 929–930. Revised and enlarged edition. Princeton: Princeton University Press, 1974.

"Fiction and Historical Reality: The Hourglass and the Sands of Time." In *Literature and History*, pp. 43–77. Los Angeles: William Andrews Clark Memorial Library, UCLA, 1974.

Paper read at a Clark Library Seminar, March 3, 1973.

"Fiction, History, and Empirical Reality." *Critical Inquiry* (December 1974), 1(2):335–360.

A quite different version of this paper was delivered at the Clark Library Seminar on Literature and History, March 3, 1973, with the title "Fiction and Historical Reality: The Hourglass and the Sands of Time."

"Geoffrey Hartman." Review of Geoffrey H. Hartman's *Beyond Formalism: Literary Essays 1958–1970*. *Contemporary Literature* (Winter 1974), 15(1): 141–144.

1975

" 'Humanist Misgivings About the Theory of Rational Choice': Comments on David Braybrooke," "Literature, Vision, and the Dilemmas of Practical Choice," "Preliminary Remarks to the Discussion of My Paper," and "A During-the-Colloquium Playful Postscript; or, a Satisfaction." In Max Black, ed., *Problems of Choice and Decision*, pp. 53–67, 398–431, 441–448, and 578–586. Proceedings of a Colloquium held in Aspen, Colorado on June 24–26, 1974, co-sponsored by the Cornell University Program on Science, Technology, and Society, and the Aspen Institute for Humanistic Studies. Ithaca, N.Y.: Cornell University Program on Science, Technology and Society, 1975.

1976

"Introduction: A Scorecard for the Critics." *Contemporary Literature* (Summer 1976), 17(3):297–326.

"Poetics Reconstructed: The Presence vs. the Absence of the Word." *New Literary History* (Winter 1976), 7(2):347–375.

A considerably reduced version of the final chapters of *Theory of Criticism: A Tradition and Its System* (1976).

"Reconsideration—The New Critics." *New Republic* (October 2, 1976), 175(14):32–34.

"Shakespeare and the Critic's Idolatry of the Word." In G. Blakemore Evans, ed., *Shakespeare: Aspects of Influence*, pp. 193–210. Harvard English Studies, 7. Cambridge and London: Harvard University Press, 1976.

"The Theoretical Contributions of Eliseo Vivas." In Henry Regnery, ed., *Viva Vivas! Essays in Honor of Eliseo Vivas, on the Occasion of His Seventy-Fifth Birthday, July 13, 1976*, pp. 37–63. Indianapolis: Liberty Press, 1976

Theory of Criticism: A Tradition and Its System. Baltimore and London: Johns Hopkins University Press, 1976.

Contents:

Preface:ix–xiv.

Part I The Problem: The Limits and Capacities Critical Theory:1–64.

1 The Vanity of Theory and Its Value:3–8.

    2 Preliminary Questions and Suggested Answers:9–37.
    3 The Critic as Person and Persona:38–64. [See "The Critic as Person and Persona" (1973).].
Part II The Humanistic Theoretical Tradition:65–175.
    4 The Deceptive Opposition Between Mimetic and Expressive Theories:67–97.
    5 Form and the Humanistic Aesthetic:98–148. [See "The Critical Legacy of Matthew Arnold; or, the Strange Brotherhood of T. S. Eliot, I. A. Richards, and Northrop Frye" (1969).]
    6 Fiction, History, and Empirical Reality: The Hourglass and the Sands of Time:149–175. [See "Fiction and Historical Reality: The Hourglass and the Sands of Time" (1974), and "Fiction, History, and Empirical Reality" (1974).]
Part III A Systematic Extension:177–245.
    7 The Aesthetic as the Anthropological: The Breath of the Word and the Weight of the World:179–206.
    8 Poetics Reconstructed: The Presence of the Poem:207–245. [See "Poetics Reconstructed: The Presence vs. the Absence of the Word" (1976).]

1977

Edited (with L. S. Dembo). *Directions for Criticism: Structuralism and Its Alternatives.* Madison, Wisc. & London: University of Wisconsin Press, 1977.
    Murray Krieger's opening essay, "Introduction: A Scorecard for the Critics," pp. 3–32, with the other essays in this volume, originally appeared as articles in *Contemporary Literature* (Summer 1976), 17(3).
See "Introduction: A Scorecard for the Critics" (1976).
The New Apologists for Poetry. Westport, Conn.: Greenwood Press, 1977.
    Reprint of the 1956 edition published by the University of Minnesota Press.
Theory of Criticism: A Tradition and Its System. Baltimore: Johns Hopkins University Press, 1977.
    A paperback reprint of the edition published by the Johns Hopkins University Press in 1976.

1978

"Literature as Illusion, as Metaphor, as Vision." In Paul Hernadi, ed., *What Is Literature?*, pp. 178–189. Bloomington, Ind.: Indiana University Press, 1978.
"Theories about Theories about *Theory of Criticism.*" *Bulletin of the Midwest Modern Language Association* (Spring 1978), 11(1):30–42.
"Truth and Troth, Fact and Faith: Accuracy to the World and Fidelity to Vision." *Journal of Comparative Literature and Aesthetics* (Vishvanatha Kaviraja Institute, Orissa, India) (1978), 1(2):51–58.
"Truth and Troth, Fact and Faith: Accuracy to the World and Fidelity to Vision." *Literary Magazine* (Irvine) (December 1978):3–5.

1979

"Literature vs. *Ecriture:* Constructions and Deconstructions in Recent Critical Theory." *Studies in the Literary Imagination* (Spring 1979), 12(1):1–17.
Poetic Presence and Illusion: Essays in Critical History and Theory. Baltimore and London: Johns Hopkins University Press, 1979.
Contents:
  Preface:xi–xv.
  I Critical History:1–135.
      1 Poetic Presence and Illusion I: Renaissance Theory and the Duplicity of Metaphor:3–27. [See "Poetic Presence and Illusion I: Renaissance Theory and the Duplicity of Metaphor" (1979)].
      2 Jacopo Mazzoni, Repository of Diverse Critical Traditions or Source of a New One?:28–38. [See "Jacopo Mazzoni, Repository of Divine Critical Traditions or Source of a New One?" (1986)].
      3 Shakespeare and the Critic's Idolatry of the Word:39–54. [See "Shakespeare and the Critic's Idolatry of the Word" (1976)].
      4 Fiction, Nature, and Literary Kinds in Johnson's Criticism of Shakespeare:55–69. [See "Fiction, Nature, and Literary Kinds in Johnson's Criticism of Shakespeare" (1971)].
      5 "Trying Experiments upon Our Sensibility": The Art of Dogma and Doubt in Eighteenth-Century Literature:70–91.
      6 The Critical Legacy of Matthew Arnold; or, The Strange Brotherhood of T. S. Eliot, I. A. Richards, and Northrop Frye:92–107. [See "The Critical Legacy of Matthew Arnold; or, the Strange Brotherhood of T. S. Eliot, I. A. Richards, and Northrop Frye" (1969)].
      7 Reconsideration—The New Critics:108–114. [See "Reconsideration—The New Critics" (1976)].
      8 The Theoretical Contributions of Eliseo Vivas:115–128. [See "The Theoretical Contributions of Eliseo Vivas" (1976)].
      9 *The Tragic Vision* Twenty Years After:129–135.
  II Critical Theory:138–322.
      10 Poetic Presence and Illusion II: Formalist Theory and the Duplicity of Metaphor:139–168. [See "Poetic Presence and Illusion II: Formalist Theory and the Duplicity of Metaphor" (1979)].
      11 Literature versus *Ecriture:* Constructions and Deconstructions in Recent Critical Theory:169–187. [See "Literature vs. *Ecriture:* Constructions and Deconstructions in Recent Critical Theory" (1979)].
      12 Literature as Illusion, as Metaphor, as Vision:188–196. [See "Literature as Illusion, as Metaphor, as Vision" (1978)].
      13 Theories about Theories about *Theory of Criticism:*197–210. [See "Theories about Theories about *Theory of Criticism*" (1978)].
      14 A Scorecard for the Critics:211–237. [See "Introduction: A Scorecard for the Critics" (1976)].

15 Literature, Criticism, and Decision Theory:238–269. [See Max Black, ed., *Problems of Choice and Decision* (1975)].

16 Mediation, Language, and Vision in the Reading of Literature:270–302. [See "Mediation, Language, and Vision in the Reading of Literature" (1969)].

17 Literary Analysis and Evaluation—and the Ambidextrous Critic:303–322. [See "Literary Analysis and Evaluation—and the Ambidextrous Critic" (1968)].

Chapters 5 and 9 appear here for the first time.

"Poetic Presence and Illusion I: Renaissance Theory and the Duplicity of Metaphor." *Critical Inquiry* (Summer 1979), 5(4):597–619.

"Poetic Presence and Illusion II: Formalist Theory and the Duplicity of Metaphor." *Boundary 2* (Fall 1979), 8(1):95–121. For diagrams inadvertently excluded from this article see "Errata," *Boundary 2* (Winter 1980), 8(2):367–368, and *Poetic Presence and Illusion: Essays in Critical History and Theory* (1979), chapter 10:139–168.

"The Recent Revolution in Theory and the Survival of the Literary Disciplines." In *The State of the Discipline, 1970s–1980s,* pp. 27–34. New York: Association of Departments of English, 1979.

A special issue of the *ADE [Association of Departments of English] Bulletin* (September–November 1979), 62.

"Reply to Norman Friedman." *Comparative Literature Studies* (September 1979), 16(3):262–264.

See review by Norman Friedman of *Theory of Criticism: A Tradition and Its System* (1976) in *Comparative Literature Studies* (June 1979), 16(2):165–167.

1981

"An Apology for Poetics." In Ira Konigsberg, ed., *American Criticism in the Post-Structuralist Age,* pp. 87–101. Michigan Studies in the Humanities, 4. Papers presented as part of a Symposium in Critical Theory held in 1979–1980 at the University of Michigan. Ann Arbor: University of Michigan Press, 1981.

Arts on the Level: The Fall of the Elite Object. Knoxville: University of Tennessee Press, 1981.

Contents:

Preface:vii–ix.

1 The Precious Object: Fetish as Aesthetic:3–24.

2 Literary Criticism: A Primary or a Secondary Art?:27–48.

3 Art and Artifact in a Commodity Society:51–71.

"Criticism as a Secondary Art." In Paul Hernadi, ed., *What Is Criticism?,* pp. 280–295. Bloomington: Indiana University Press, 1981.

A condensed version of *Arts on the Level: The Fall of the Elite Object* (1981), chapter 2:27–48.

"Tragedy and the Tragic Vision," and "*The Tragic Vision* Twenty Years After." In Robert W. Corrigan, ed., *Tragedy: Vision and Form,* pp. 30–41, 42–46. New York: Harper & Row, 1981.

See "Tragedy and the Tragic Vision" (1958), *The Tragic Vision* (1960),
(1973) chapter 1, pp. 1–21, and *Poetic Presence and Illusion: Essays in Critical
History and Theory* (1979), chapter 9, pp. 129–135.
" 'A Waking Dream': The Symbolic Alternative to Allegory." In Morton W. Bloom-
field, ed., *Allegory, Myth, and Symbol,* pp. 1–22. Harvard English Studies, 9.
Cambridge and London: Harvard University Press, 1981.

1982

"The Arts and the Idea of Progress." In Gabriel A. Almond, Marvin Chodorow, and
Roy Harvey Pearce, eds., *Progress and Its Discontents,* pp. 449–469. Papers based
on a Conference sponsored by the Western Center of the American Academy of
Arts and Sciences, held in February 1979, in Palo Alto, California. Berkeley, Los
Angeles, and London: University of California Press, 1982.
"Feodor Mikhailovich Dostoevski." In Laurie Lanzen Harries, ed., *Nineteenth-Cen-
tury Literature Criticism,* 2:199. Detroit: Gale Research, 1982.
See *The Tragic Vision* (1960), (1973), pp. 209–227.
"Poetic Presence and Illusion II: Formalist Theory and the Duplicity of Metaphor."
In William V. Spanos, Paul A. Bove, and Daniel O'Hara, eds., *The Question of
Textuality: Strategies of Reading in Contemporary American Criticism,* pp. 95–121.
Bloomington: Indiana University Press, 1982.
See "Poetic Presence and Illusion II: Formalist Theory and the Duplicity of
Metaphor" (1979), and *Poetic Presence and Illusion: Essays in Critical History and
Theory* (1979), chapter 10:139–168.
"Presentation and Representation in the Renaissance Lyric: The Net of Words and
the Escape of the Gods." In John D. Lyons and Stephen G. Nichols, eds.,
Mimesis: From Mirror to Method, Augustine to Descartes, pp. 110–131. Hanover,
NH: University Press of New England, 1982.
Teoria Criticii: Traditie si sistem. Introduction by Radu Surdulescu. Bucharest: Uni-
vers, 1982.
Romanian translation by Radu Surdulescu of *Theory of Criticism: A Tradition
and Its System* (1976).
Teorija Kritike. Introduction by Nikola Koljevic. Belgrade: Nolit, 1982.
Serbo-Croatian translation by Svetozar M. Ignjacevic of *Theory of Criticism: A
Tradition and Its System* (1976).
"Theories about Theories about *Theory of Criticism.*" In Paul Hernadi, ed., *The
Horizon of Literature,* pp. 319–336. Lincoln: University of Nebraska Press,
1982.
See "Theories about Theories about *Theory of Criticism*" (1978), and *Poetic
Presence and Illusion: Essays in Critical History and Theory* (1979), chapter 13:197–
210.

1983

"Both Sides Now." *New Orleans Review* (Spring 1983), 10(1):18–23.
"I. A. Richards." In Sharon R. Gunton, ed., *Contemporary Literary Criticism,* 24:391–
392. Detroit: Gale Research, 1983.

See *The New Apologists for Poetry* (1956), chapter 3:57–63.

"In the Wake of Morality: The Thematic Underside of Recent Theory." *New Literary History* (Autumn 1983), 15(1):119–136.

"Literary Theory in the University: A Survey." *New Literary History* (Winter 1983), 14(2):432–433.

"A Matter of Distinction: An Interview with Murray Krieger." Conducted by Richard Berg. *New Orleans Review* (Spring 1983), 10(1):48–62.

"Northrop Frye." In Sharon R. Gunton, ed., *Contemporary Literary Criticism,* 24:223–225. Detroit: Gale Research, 1983.

See "Northrop Frye and Contemporary Criticism: Ariel and the Spirit of Gravity" (1966), and *The Play and Place of Criticism* (1967), chapter 15:221–237.

"Orpheus *mit Glück:* The Deceiving Gratifications of Presence." *Theatre Journal* (October 1983), 35(3):295–305.

Words about Words about Words: The "What" and "Why" of Literary Theory. Irvine: University of California, Irvine, 1983.

Distinguished Faculty Lecture delivered on February 24, 1983.

1984

"The Ambiguities of Representation and Illusion: an E. H. Gombrich Retrospective." *Critical Inquiry* (December 1984), 11(2):181–194.

"A Humanity Within the Humanities: Literature Among the Discourses." *Journal of Literary Criticism* (Allahabad, India) (Summer 1984), 1(1).

"The Literary Privilege of Evaluation." In Joseph P. Strelka, ed., *Literary Theory and Criticism: Festschrift in Honor of René Wellek,* part I: Theory, pp. 369–391. Berne, Frankfurt and New York: Lang, 1984.

"Literature vs. *Ecriture:* Constructions and Deconstructions in Recent Critical Theory." In Victor A. Kramer, ed., *American Critics at Work: Examinations of Contemporary Literary Theory,* pp. 27–48. Troy, NY: Whitston, 1984.

Revised version of "Literature vs. *Ecriture:* Coonstructions and Deconstructions in Recent Critical Theory" (1979).

"Post-New-Critical Fashions in Theory." *Indian Journal of American Studies* (ASRC, Hyderabad, India) (July 1984), 14(2):189–206.

This is a revised version of remarks delivered at the American Studies Research Centre in Hyderabad, India on January 31, 1984.

"Words about Words about Words: Theory, Criticism, and the Literary Text." *Academe: Bulletin of AAUP* (March–April 1984), 70(1):17–24.

The article is adapted from the Distinguished Faculty Lecture delivered at the University of California, Irvine on February 24, 1983.

See *Words about Words about Words: the "What" and "Why" of Literary Theory* (1983).

1985

"Optics and Aesthetic Perception: A Rebuttal." *Critical Inquiry* (March 1985), 11(3):502–508.

1986

"Analyse und Wertung—und der Zwiehandige Literaturkritiker." In Jürgen Schlae-
ger, ed., *Kritik in der Krise: Theorie der amerikanischen Literaturkritik,* pp. 78–98.
Munich: Fink, 1986.
    German translation by Margit Smuda and Sabine Deitmer of "Literary Analy-
    sis and Evaluation—and the Ambidextrous Critic" (1968).
"An Apology for Poetics." In Hazard Adams and Leroy Searle, eds, *Critical Theory
Since 1965,* pp. 534–542. Tallahassee: University Presses of Florida, Florida State
University Press, 1986.
    See "An Apology for Poetics" (1981).
"Both Sides Now." In Bruce Henricksen, ed., *Murray Krieger and Contemporary
Critical Theory,* pp. 42–55. Irvine Studies in the Humanities. New York: Colum-
bia University Press, 1986.
    See "Both Sides Now" (1983).
"Literary Invention and the Impulse to Theoretical Change; 'Or Whether Revolution
Be the Same.' " *New Literary History* (Autumn 1986), 18(1):191–208.
    Revised version of next item.
"Literary Invention and the Impulse to Theoretical Change: 'Whether Revolution Be
the Same.' " In Miklós Szabolcsi, József Kovács, Matild Gulyás, eds., *Change in
Language and Literature,* pp. 115–136. Proceedings of the 16th Triennial Con-
gress of the Federation Internationale des Langues et Litteratures Modernes
[FILLM], August 22–27, 1984, held in Budapest. Budapest: Akadémiai Kiadó,
1986.
"A Matter of Distinction: An Interview with Murray Krieger." (Interview conducted
by Richard Berg) In Bruce Henricksen, ed., *Murray Krieger and Contemporary
Critical Theory,* pp. 198–230. Irvine Studies in the Humanities. New York:
Columbia University Press, 1986.
    See "A Matter of Distinction: An Interview with Murray Krieger" (1983).
"Murray Krieger at Konstanz: A Colloquy Chaired by Wolfgang Iser." (Participants:
Murray Krieger, Ulrich Gaier, Anselm Haverkamp, Wolfgang Iser, Hans Robert
Jauss, Jurgen Schlaeger, Gabrille Schwab.) In Bruce Henricksen, ed., *Murray
Krieger and Contemporary Critical Theory,* pp. 231–270. Irvine Studies in the
Humanities. New York: Columbia University Press, 1986.
"Presentation and Representation in the Renaissance Lyric: The Net of Words and
the Escape of the Gods." In Richard Machin and Christopher Norris, eds., *Post-
Structuralist Readings of English Poetry,* pp. 20–37. Cambridge: Cambridge Uni-
versity Press, 1986.
    See "Presentation and Representation in the Renaissance Lyric: The Net of
    Words and the Escape of the Gods" (1982).

1987

Editor. *The Aims of Representation: Subject/Text/History.* Introduction by Murray
Krieger. Irvine Studies in the Humanities. New York: Columbia University Press,
1987.

"Introduction: The Literary, the Textual, the Social," In Murray Krieger, ed., *The Aims of Representation: Subject/Text/History,* pp. 1–22. Irvine Studies in the Humanities. New York: Columbia University Press, 1987.

"Poetry as Art, Language as Aesthetic Medium." In Doug Bolling, ed., *Philosophy and Literature,* pp. 5–34. Art and Philosophy, 3. New York: Haven, 1987.

  Lead essay of the volume to which nine philosophers and critics respond. See Part 2 of this bibliography.

"Post-New-Critical Fashions in Theory." In S. Viswanathan, C. T. Indra, T. Sriraman, eds., *Critical Essays: A Presentation Volume for Professor V. S. Seturaman,* pp. 36–61. New Delhi: Macmillan India, 1987.

  See "Post-New-Critical Fashions in Theory" (1984).

"Die Unwandlung von Geschichte in Utopie in Shakespeares *Sonetten." Shakespeare-Jahrbuch* (1987), 123:42–53.

  German translation by Klaus Schirrmeister of "The Conversion from History to Utopia in Shakespeare's *Sonnets*" (1988). See *Words about Words about Words: Theory, Criticism, and the Literary Text* (1988), chapter 13:242–255.

1988

Words about Words about Words: Theory, Criticism, and the Literary Text. Baltimore, MD and London: Johns Hopkins University Press, 1988.

  Contents:

  Preface:ix–xii.

  I Theory and Institutions: Critical Movements and Academic Structures:2–104.

    1 Words *about* Words *about* Words: Theory, Criticism, and the Literary Text:3–19. [A revised version of *Words about Words about Words: The 'What' and 'Why' of Literary Theory* (1983). See "Words about Words about Words: Theory, Criticism, and the Literary Text" (1984)].

    2 The Arts and the Idea of Progress:20–42. [See "The Arts and the Idea of Progress" (1982)].

    3 From Theory to Thematics: The Ideological Underside of Recent Theory:43–63. [A substantially revised version of "In the Wake of Morality: The Thematic Underside of Recent Theory" (1983)].

    4 Literary Invention, Critical Fashion, and the Impulse to Theoretical Change; "Or Whether Revolution Be the Same":64–89. [See "Literary Invention and the Impulse to Theoretical Change; "Or, Whether Revolution Be the Same" (1986)].

    5 A Meditation on a Critical Theory Institute:90–104.

  II Critical Positions: Self-definition and Other Definitions:105–203.

    6 An Apology for Poetics:107–119. [See "An Apology for Poetics" (1981)].

    7 A Colloquy on "An Apology for Poetics":120–152. [See "Murray Krieger at Konstanz: A Colloquy Chaired by Wolfgang Iser" (1986)].

    8 The Literary Privilege of Evaluation:153–171. [See "The Literary Privilege of Evaluation" (1984)].

    9 An E. H. Gombrich Retrospective: The Ambiguities of Representation and

Illusion:172–192. (See "An E. H. Gombrich Retrospective: The Ambiguities of Representation and Illusion" (1984)].

10 "Both Sides Now":193–203. [See "Both Sides Now" (1983), (1986)].

III Reconsideration of Special Texts for Special Reasons:206–288.

11 Presentation and Representation in the Renaissance Lyric: The Net of
Words and the Escape of the Gods:207–225. [See "Presentation and
Representation in the Renaissance Lyric: The Net of Words and the
Escape of the Gods" (1982)].

12 A Humanity in the Humanities: Literature among the Discourses:226–
241. [See "A Humanity Within the Humanities: Literature Among the
Discourses" (1984)].

13 The Conversion from History to Utopia in Shakespeare's *Sonnets:*242–
255.

14 Orpheus *mit Gluck:* The Deceiving Gratific(a)tions of Presence:256–270.
[See "Orpheus *mit Gluck:* The Deceiving Gratifications of Presence"
(1983)].

15 "A Waking Dream": The Symbolic Alternative to Allegory:271–288.
[See " 'A Waking Dream': The Symbolic Alternative to Allegory" (1981)].

1989

"From Theory to Thematics." In Rajnath, ed., *Deconstruction: A Critique.* Basing-
stoke: Macmillan, 1989.

To Be Published

"Coda: The Exhilarations—and Exasperations—of *Ekphrasis* as a Subject." In Michael
Riffaterre, ed., *The Poetics of Ekphrasis.* Baltimore: Johns Hopkins University
Press.

Selected Critical References to Murray Krieger and His Writings

Abdulla, Adnan K. *Catharsis in Literature,* pp. 89, 92–96, 139*n*6, 142*n*5, 148*nn*22,
23, 143*nn*9, 10, 11, 20, 21, 22, 23. Bloomington: Indiana University Press,
1985.

Ackerman, Stephen J. "The Vocation of Pope's *Eloisa.*" *Studies in English Literature
1500–1900* (Summer 1979), 19(3):446–448.

Adams, Hazard. "Criticism: Whence and Whither?" Review of *The New Apologists for
Poetry* (1956). *American Scholar* (Spring 1959), 28(2):226–228.

——"Hazard Adams on Literary Criticism." Review of *Theory of Criticism: A Tradition and Its System* (1976). *New Republic* (November 27, 1976), 175(22):30.

——"Introduction: The Gentle Behemoth; or, The Illusionist of Truth; or, The

Bourgeois (with a Trace of Existentialism) Gentilhomme; or, The Experienced Uncle Toby; and, finally, Practical Kriegerism." *New Orleans Review* (Spring 1983), 10(1):5–7.

——"Introduction: The Gentle Behemoth." In Bruce Henricksen, ed., *Murray Krieger and Contemporary Critical Theory*, pp. 1–18. Irvine Studies in the Humanities. New York: Columbia University Press, 1986.

——Review of *A Window to Criticism: Shakespeare's 'Sonnets' and Modern Poetics* (1964). *Criticism* (Spring 1965), 7(2):190–193.

Adams, Hazard and Leroy Searle. "Murray Krieger." In Hazard Adams and Leroy Searle, eds., *Critical Theory Since 1965*, p. 534. Tallahassee: University Presses of Florida, Florida State University Press, 1986.

Armstrong, Paul B. "Murray Krieger." In Gregory S. Jay, ed., *Modern American Critics Since 1955*, pp. 213–220. Dictionary of Literary Biography, 67. Detroit: Gale Research, A Bruccoli Clark Layman Book, 1988.

Arnavon, C. Review of *The New Apologists for Poetry* (1956). *Etudes Anglaises* (July–September 1958), 11(3):274–275.

Arnold, Aerol. "Window to Criticism." Review of *A Window to Criticism: Shakespeare's 'Sonnets' and Modern Poetics* (1964). *Personalist* (Summer 1965), 46(3):401–403.

Avadanei, Stefan. Review of *Teoria criticii: Traditie si sistem* (1982). *Cronica* (Jassy, Romania) (August 12, 1983):10.

Bache, William B. Review of *Arts on the Level: The Fall of the Elite Object* (1981). *Modern Fiction Studies* (Summer 1982), 28(2):345–346.

——Review of *Poetic Presence and Illusion: Essays in Critical History and Theory* (1979). *Modern Fiction Studies* (Summer 1981), 27(2):386–387.

Barber, C. L. "Full to Overflowing." Review of Stephen Booth's *Shakespeare's Sonnets*. *New York Review of Books* (April 1978), 25(5):37.

Barfoot, C. C. Review of *Theory of Criticism: A Tradition and Its System* (1976). *English Studies* (December 1977), 58(6):548–549.

Bateson, Frederic. *A Guide to English Literature*, p. 199. Garden City: Doubleday, 1965.

Battersby, James L. *Rational Praise and Natural Lamentation: Johnson, "Lycidas," and the Principles of Criticism*, pp. 13, 18–19, 21, 24, 109–123, 246nn4, 10, 11, 12, 256nn7–12, 257nn16, 18–20, 22–27, 258nn28, 29, 270. Rutherford, N.J.: Fairleigh Dickinson University Press; London: Associated University Presses, 1980.

Berry, Francis, Review of *The Play and Place of Criticism* (1967). *Review of English Studies* (N.S.) (May 1969), 20(78):246–247.

——Review of *Theory of Criticism: A Tradition and Its System* (1976). *Review of English Studies* (N.S.) (November 1977), 28(112):507–508.

Bertens, Hans. Review of Frank Lentricchia's *After the New Criticism. Revue de Litterature Comparée* (October–December 1985), 59(4):459, 460.

Bertocci, Angelo P. Review of *The Play and Place of Criticism* (1967). *Comparative Literature Studies* (September 1968), 5(3):355–359.

Bierman, Ronald. "Shakespeare: Some Recent Books." Review of *A Window to*

Criticism: Shakespeare's 'Sonnets' and Modern Poetics (1964). *Kenyon Review* (Summer 1964), 26(3):566.

Black, Joel D. "Allegory Unveiled." Review of Morton W. Bloomfield, ed., *Allegory, Myth, and Symbol* (1981). *Poetics Today* (1983), 4(1):117–119.

Blissett, William. Review of *Northrop Frye in Modern Criticism* (1966). *University of Toronto Quarterly* (July 1967), 36(4):414.

Blocker, H. Gene. "The Medium of Poetry and the Aesthetic Tradition." In Doug Bolling, ed., *Philosophy and Literature*, pp. 137–156. Art and Philosophy, 3. New York: Haven, 1987.

Bollas, Christopher. "The Aesthetic Moment and the Search for Transformation." In J. J. Feldstein, ed., *Annual of Psychoanalysis, 1978*, pp. 385–388, 393, 394n. New York: International University Press, 1978.

Bolling, Doug. "Introduction to the Volume." In Doug Bolling, ed., *Philosophy and Literature*, pp. 1–4. Art and Philosophy, 3. New York: Haven, 1987.

   Nine philosophers and critics respond to Krieger's "Poetry as Art, Language as Aesthetic Medium." For their contributions see the entries under the names H. Gene Blocker, Doug Bolling, George Dickie, Martin Donougho, Charles L. Griswold, Jr., W. E. Kennick, Joseph Margolis, Thomas G. Pavel and Steven David Ross.

Booth, Wayne C. *The Rhetoric of Fiction*, p. 95n12. Chicago and London: University of Chicago Press, 1961.

——*A Rhetoric of Irony*, p. 193n. Chicago: University of Chicago Press, 1974.

Borklund, Elmer. "Krieger, Murray." In *Contemporary Literary Critics*, pp. 318–323. London: St. James Press; New York: St. Martin's Press, 1977. 2d. ed., pp. 341–346. London: Macmillan, 1982.

——Review of *The Tragic Vision: Variations on a Theme in Literary Interpretation* (1960). *Modern Philology* (May 1963), 60(4):303–306.

Brill, Hans. Review of *Arts on the Level: The Fall of the Elite Object* (1981). *Leonardo* (Autumn 1983), 16(4):329–330.

Brooks, Cleanth. "The State of Criticism: A Sampling." Review of *The New Apologists for Poetry* (1957). *Sewanee Review* (Summer 1957), 65(3):495–498.

Brown, Frank Burch. Review of *Poetic Presence and Illusion: Essays in Critical History and Theory* (1979). *Religious Studies Review* (April 1983), 9(2):165.

Bruckmann, Patricia Carr. " 'Religious Hope and Resignation': The Process of *Eloisa to Abelard.*" *English Studies in Canada* (Summer 1977), 3(2):155: 158–159, 161, 163nn21, 26.

Bryant, Donald Cross. "Introduction—Uses of Rhetoric in Criticism." In Donald C. Bryant, ed., *Papers in Rhetoric and Poetic*, p. 8. Iowa City: University of Iowa Press, 1965.

Buchan, A. M. Review of *A Window to Criticism: Shakespeare's 'Sonnets' and Modern Poetics* (1964). *St. Louis Post-Dispatch* (April 12, 1964):4D.

Burke, Daniel. Review of *The Play and Place of Criticism* (1967). *Thought* (Spring 1968), 43(168):127–128.

Burke, Fidelian. Review of *The New Apologists for Poetry* (1956). *Literature East and West* (Spring 1957), 3(4):61–63.

Cain, William E. *The Crisis in Criticism: Theory, Literature, and Reform in English Studies*, pp. 104, 117, 221, 222, 224, 290n2. Baltimore and London: Johns Hopkins University Press, 1984.
——Review of Frank Lentricchia's *After the New Criticism. Western Humanities Review* (Summer 1981), 35(2):193, 194, 195.
——Review of Victor A. Kramer, ed., *American Critics at Work: Examinations of Contemporary Literary Theory* (1984). *Philosophy and Literature* (October 1986), 10(2):337–338.
Carroll, David. "History as Writing." Review of Jacques Derrida's *Of Grammatology. Clio* (Spring 1978), 7(3):459n8.
Clark, Michael. "The Lure of the Text, or Uncle Toby's Revenge." *New Orleans Review* (Spring 1983), 10(1):34–47. Reprinted in Bruce Henricksen, ed., *Murray Krieger and Contemporary Critical Theory*, pp. 135–156. Irvine Studies in the Humanities. New York: Columbia University Press, 1986.
Colie, Rosalie L. *'My Echoing Song': Andrew Marvell's Poetry of Criticism*, pp. 4n1, 100, 100n. Princeton, N.J.: Princeton University Press, 1970.
——*Paradoxia Epidemica: The Renaissance Tradition of Paradox*, pp. 99n8, 130n39, 275n5, 367n12. Princeton, N.J.: Princeton University Press, 1966.
——*Shakespeare's Living Art*, pp. 50n15, 57n29, 144n10, 361n24. Princeton, N.J.: Princeton University Press, 1974.
Cox, R. Gordon. Review of *Northrop Frye in Modern Criticism* (1966). *British Journal of Aesthetics* (January 1968), 8(1):76–79.
Crane, R. S. *The Languages of Criticism and the Structure of Poetry*, pp. 91, 199n102. Toronto: University of Toronto Press, 1953.
Cruttwell, Patrick. "Shakespeare: The Anniversary Year in Retrospect." Review of *A Window to Criticism: Shakespeare's 'Sonnets' and Modern Poetics* (1964). *Hudson Review* (Winter 1964–65), 17(4):497–498.
Davenport, William H. Review of *The New Apologists for Poetry* (1956). *Personalist* (Summer 1957), 38(3):318–319.
Davey, E. R. Review of *The Classic Vision: The Retreat from Extremity in Modern Literature* (1971). *Journal of European Studies* (September 1972), 2(3):287.
Davidson, James W. "Criticism and Social Action." (Part 1) Review of Frank Lentricchia's *After the New Criticism. Papers on Language and Literature* (Winter 1982), 18(4):442, 443, 444, 447–448, 452–453.
Dembo, L. S. "Introduction and Perspective." In L. S. Dembo, ed., *Criticism: Speculative and Analytical Essays*, pp. 3–8. Madison: University of Wisconsin Press, 1968.
Dickie, George. "Radical Disinterest." In Doug Bolling, ed., *Philosophy and Literature*, pp. 129–136. Art and Philosophy, 3, New York: Haven, 1987.
Donoghue, Denis. "Critique of Criticism." Review of *Theory of Criticism: A Tradition and Its System* (1976). *Times Higher Education Supplement* (March 4, 1977), 280:22.
——"In Their Masters' Steps." Review of *Words about Words about Words: Theory, Criticism, and the Literary Text. TLS [Times Literary Supplement] (December 16–22, 1988), 4472:1400.

——"The Onward March of Obsolescence." Review of Grant Webster's The Republic of Letters. TLS [Times Literary Supplement] (July 11, 1980), 4033:775.

Donougho, Martin. "Framing the Medium." In Doug Bolling, ed., Philosophy and Literature, pp. 35–52. Art and Philosophy, 3. New York: Haven, 1987.

Doubrovsky, Serge. The New Criticism in France, pp. 16–17, 24–37. Derek Coltmann, trans. Chicago: University of Chicago Press, 1973.

Douglas, Wallace D. Review of The New Apologists for Poetry (1956). College English (January 1957), 18(4):231.

Emerson. Donald. Review of The Tragic Vision: Variations on a Theme in Literary Interpretation (1960). Prairie Schooner (June 1961), 35(2):172–173.

Fekete, John. The Critical Twilight: Explorations in the Ideology of Anglo-American Literary Theory from Eliot to McLuhan, pp. 21, 43, 44, 49, 121, 224n26, 229nn1, 3, 231nn15, 18, 248n45. London, Henley & Boston: Routledge & Kegan Paul, 1978.

Foakes, R. A. Review of A Window to Criticism: Shakespeare's 'Sonnets' and Modern Poetics (1964). English (Autumn 1964), 15(87):112.

Foster, Richard. The New Romantics: A Reappraisal of the New Criticism, pp. 14, 26–27, 42, 86, 134, 149–150, 211n2, 214n25, 223n1, 227n47. Bloomington: Indiana University Press, 1962.

Fowlie, Wallace. "New Critics on Verse . . ." Review of The New Apologists for Poetry (1956). Saturday Review (May 19, 1956), 39(20):29.

Free, William J. "Murray Krieger and the Place of Poetry." Georgia Review (Summer 1968), 22(2):236–246.

Friedman, Norman. Review of Theory of Criticism: A Tradition and Its System (1976). Comparative Literature Studies (June 1979), 16(2):165–167.
    See Krieger's "Reply to Norman Friedman" (1979).

Fry, Paul. Review of Theory of Criticism: A Tradition and Its System (1976). Structuralist Review (Spring 1978), 1:110–115.

Frye, Northrop. "On Value Judgments." In L. S. Dembo, ed., Criticism: Speculative and Analytical Essays, pp. 37, 39. Madison and London: University of Wisconsin Press, 1968.

Fubini, Enrico. Review of "Contextualism Was Ambitious" (1962). Rivista di Estetica (Italy) (May–August 1963), 8(3):309.

Gellrich, Jesse. "Deconstructing Allegory." Genre (Fall 1985), 8(3):198–201, 211nn5, 6, 9, 10, 11, 12, 212n14.

Gerhart, Mary. Review of Theory of Criticism: A Tradition and Its System (1976). Religious Studies Review (July 1977), 3(3):193.

Glicksberg, Charles Irving. Review of The Tragic Vision: Variations on a Theme in Literary Interpretation (1960). Arizona Quarterly (Summer 1961), 17(2):187–190.

——The Tragic Vision in Twentieth-Century Literature, pp. xiv, 157, 158n5, 159n9, 167, 168n10, 180n12. Carbondale: Southern Illinois University Press; London and Amsterdam: Feffer & Simons, 1983.

Goldsmith, Arnold L. American Literary Criticism: 1905–1965, pp. 103, 107, 114–115, 131, 133–134, 180nn3, 20, 184n3. Boston: Twayne, 1979.

Gombrich, E. H. "Representation and Misrepresentation." *Critical Inquiry* (December 1984), 11(2):195–201.
A response to Krieger's "The Ambiguities of Representation and Illusion: An E. H. Gombrich Retrospective" (1984). For Krieger's reply see "Optics and Aesthetic Perception: A Rebuttal" (1985).

Goodhart, Sandor. "After *The Tragic Vision:* Krieger and Lentricchia, Criticism and Crisis." In Bruce Hendricksen, ed., *Murray Krieger and Contemporary Critical Theory,* pp. 179–197. Irvine Studies in the Humanities. New York: Columbia University Press, 1986.

Graff, Gerald. *Poetic Statement and Critical Dogma,* pp. 15n28, 16, 19, 21–23, 75–76, 78, 90, 91n8, 103, 106–109, 139n4, 146, 180, 182. Evanston, Ill.: Northwestern University Press, 1970.

——"Tongue-in-Cheek Humanism: A Response to Murray Krieger." *ADE Bulletin* (Fall 1981), 69:18–21.
A response to Krieger's "The Recent Revolution in Theory and the Survival of Literary Disciplines" (1979).

Gras, Vernon. Review of *Directions for Criticism: Structuralism and Its Alternatives* (1977), and *Theory of Criticism: A Tradition and Its System (1976). Papers on Language & Literature* (Summer 1978), 14(3):369–371.

Griffin, Lloyd W. Review of *Northrop Frye in Modern Criticism* (1966). *Library Journal* (September 1, 1966), 91(15):3951–3952.

——Review of *The Tragic Vision: Variations on a Theme in Literary Interpretation* (1960). *Library Journal* (November 15, 1960), 85:4146–4147.

Griffith, Ben W. Review of *The New Apologists for Poetry* (1956). *Savannah Morning News* (Georgia) (December 9, 1956):20.

Grigorescu, Irina. Review of *Teoria criticii: Traditie si sistem* (1982). *Romania Literara* (Bucharest) (August 18, 1983):23.

Griswold, Charles L., Jr. "Irony and Aesthetic Language in Plato's Dialogues." In Doug Bolling, ed., *Philosophy and Literature,* pp. 69–99. Art and Philosophy, 3. New York: Haven, 1987.

Gross, Harvey. *The Contived Corridor: History and Fatality in Modern Literature,* pp. 45, 193n6. Ann Arbor, MI: University of Michigan Press, 1971.

Gudas, Fabian. Review of *Theory of Criticism: A Tradition and Its System* (1976). *Journal of Aesthetics and Art Criticism* (Summer 1977), 35(4):480–482.

Guenther, Charles. "A Critic of Critics." Review of *The New Apologists for Poetry* (1956). *St. Louis Post-Dispatch* (November 19, 1956), 78(320):2B.

Hamilton, Alice. Review of *Northrop Frye in Modern Criticism* (1966). *Dalhousie Review* (Spring 1967), 47(1):105–107.

Hamm, Victor M. Review of *The New Apologists for Poetry* (1956). *Renascence* (Autumn 1957), 10(1):50–52.

Hardison, O. B., Jr. "Krieger Agonistes." Review of *Theory of Criticism: A Tradition and Its System* (1976). *Sewanee Review* (Fall 1977), 85(4): cxv–cxviii.

Harries, Karston. Review of *Arts on the Level: The Fall of the Elite Object* (1981). *Journal of Aesthetics and Art Criticism* (Spring 1982), 40(3):333–334.

Harrison, G. B. "Bardolatry, 1964: Hoopla and Wit." Review of *A Window to*

Criticism: Shakespeare's 'Sonnets' and Modern Poetics (1964). *New York Herald Tribune Book Week* (April 26, 1964), 1(33):8.

Hart, Thomas R. Review of *A Window to Criticism: Shakespeare's 'Sonnets' and Modern Poetics* (1964). *Books Abroad* (Spring 1965), 39:211–212.

Hartman, Geoffrey H. "Beyond Formalism." In Gregory T. Polletta, ed., *Issues in Contemporary Literary Criticism*, p. 173n3. Boston, MA: Little, Brown, 1973.

——*Criticism in the Wilderness: The Study of Literature Today*, pp. 25, 241n9. New Haven, and London: Yale University Press, 1980.

——"The Culture of Criticism." *PMLA* (May 1984), 99(3):392n17.

Harvey, W. J. "Not Enough Muddle?" Review of *Northrop Frye in Modern Criticism* (1966). *Listener* (January 5, 1967), 77(1971):32.

Hassan, Ihab. "The Critic as Innovator: A Paracritical Strip in X Frames." *Chicago Review* (Winter 1977). 28(3):22–23n4.

——"The Critical Scene: Issues in Postmodern American Criticism." *Dutch Quarterly Review of Anglo-American Letters* (1987), 17(3):169n23.

——*The Dismemberment of Orpheus: Toward a Postmodern Literature*, 2d ed., p. 277n53. Madison: University of Wisconsin Press, 1982.

——"Frontiers of Criticism: Metaphors of Silence." In David H. Malone, ed., *The Frontiers of Criticism*, p. 49. Los Angeles: Hennessey and Ingalls, 1974.

——"Making Sense: The Trials of Postmodern Discourse." *New Literary History* (Winter 1987), 18(2):448, 458nn29, 36, 459n40.

——"Pluralism in Postmodern Perspective." *Critical Inquiry* (Spring 1986), 12(3):512.

——*The Right Promethean Fire: Imagination, Science and Cultural Change*, pp. 20, 73. Urbana: University of Illinois Press, 1980.

Hawkes, Terence. "The Anti-Historical Virus." Review of Frank Lentricchia's *After the New Criticism. TLS [Times Literary Supplement]* (April 17, 1981), 4072:444.

Heller, Scott. "Humanities Institutes Signal Resurgent Interest in Field: Centers are Intellectual Home to Many Scholars." *Chronicle of Higher Education* (May 18, 1988), 34(36):A4–A5, A8.
    The contributions by Hazard Adams, Michael Clark, Sandor Goodhart, Bruce Henricksen, James Huffman, Wolfgang Iser, Vincent Leitch, Wesley Morris, Herman Rapaport, Mark Rose, and Adena Rosmarin to this volume can be found in their proper alphabetical place in this part of the bibliography.

Henricksen, Bruce, ed. *Murray Krieger and Contemporary Critical Theory.* Irvine Studies in the Humanities. New York: Columbia University Press, 1986.

——"Murray Krieger and the Question of History." In Bruce Henricksen, ed., *Murray Krieger and Contemporary Critical Theory*, pp. 119–134. Irvine Studies in the Humanities. New York: Columbia University Press, 1986.

Herring, Henry D. "Literature, Concepts, and Knowledge." *New Literary History* (Autumn 1986), 18(1):174–175, 176, 177, 179–180, 181–182, 188, 189nn3, 4, 12.

Hertz, Neil. "Balancing Acts." Review of *The Play and Place of Criticism* (1967). *Southern Review* (Spring 1970), 6(2):553–554.

Hirsch, David H. "Penelope's Web." Review of Frank Lentricchia's *After the New Criticism*. *Sewanee Review* (Winter 1982), 90(1):126, 127, 128.

Hirsch, E. D., Jr. *The Aims of Interpretation*, pp. 95, 163n1. Chicago: and London: University of Chicago Press, 1976.

Hoeniger, F. David. Review of *Northrop Frye in Modern Criticism* (1966). *Arcadia* (1970), 5(1):94–98.

Holland, Norman. *The Dynamics of Literary Response*, pp. 128, 349n15. New York & London: Norton, 1975.

——"Psychological Depths in 'Dover Beach'." In Jonathan Middlebrook, ed., *Matthew Arnold: 'Dover Beach'*, pp. 96n1, 97–99. Columbus, Ohio: Merrill, 1970.

Huffman, James. "Murray Krieger and the Impasse in Contextualist Poetics." In Bruce Henricksen, ed., *Murray Krieger and Contemporary Critical Theory*, pp. 78–95. Irvine Studies in the Humanities. New York: Columbia University Press, 1986.

Iser, Wolfgang. "Murray Krieger at Konstanz: A Colloquy Chaired by Wolfgang Iser." (Participants: Wolfgang Iser, Murray Krieger, Ulrich Gaier, Anselm Haverkamp, Hans Robert Jauss, Jurgen Schlaeger, Gabriele Schwab.) In Bruce Henricksen, ed., *Murray Krieger and Contemporary Critical Theory*, pp. 231–270. Irvine Studies in the Humanities. New York: Columbia University Press, 1986.

——"The Reading Process: A Phenomenological Approach." In Vassilis Lambropoulos and David Neal Miller, eds., *Twentieth-Century Literary Theory: An Introductory Anthology*, p. 399n19. Intersections. Philosophy and Critical Theory. Albany, N.Y.: State University of New York Press, 1987.

Jameson, Frederic. *The Political Unconscious: Narrative as a Socially Dynamic Act*, p. 209. Ithaca, N.Y.: Cornell University Press, 1981.

Jeffrey, David K. " 'A Strange Itch in the Flesh of a Nun': The Dramatic Movement and Imagery of Pope's 'Eloisa to Abelard.' " *Ball State University Forum* (Autumn 1975), 16(4):28–35.

Joseph, Terri Brint. "Murray Krieger as Pre- and Post-Deconstructionist." *New Orleans Review* (Winter 1985), 12(4):18–26.

Kalmey, Robert. "Rhetoric, Language, and Structure in *Eloisa to Abelard*." *Eighteenth-Century Studies* (Winter 1971–1972), 5(2):315–318.
    See Krieger's "Reply to Robert Kalmey" (1971).

Kartiganer, Donald M. "The Criticism of Murray Krieger: The Expansions of Contextualism." *Boundary 2* (Spring 1974). 2(3):584–607.

Kaufmann, U. Milo. Review of *A Window to Criticism: Shakespeare's 'Sonnets' and Modern Poetics* (1964). *JEGP* (July 1966), 65(3):592–595.

Kennick, W. E. "On a Putative Peculiarity of Language as a Medium of Art." In Doug Bolling, ed., *Philosophy and Literature*, pp. 101–115. Art and Philosophy, 3. New York: Haven, 1987.

Kessel, Barbara Bailey. "Free, Classless, and Urbane?" In Louis Kampf and Paul Lauter, eds., *The Politics of Literature: Dissenting Essays in the Teaching of English*, pp. 188–192, 193n5. New York: Pantheon Books, 1972.

Koljevic, Nikola. "Krigoreva Sinteza Esteticke Tradicije." ["Krieger's Synthesis of the

Aesthetic Tradition."] In Murray Krieger, *Teorije Kritike*, pp. 9–20. Belgrade: Nolit, 1982.

Preface to the Serbo-Croatian translation (by Svetozar M. Ignjacevic) of *Theory of Criticism: A Tradition and Its System* (1976).

Kramer, Victor A. "Critics at Work: Contemporary Literary Theory—Comment." *Studies in the Literary Imagination* (Spring 1979), 12(1):v–viii.

——"Introduction." In Victor A. Kramer, ed., *American Critics at Work: Examinations of Contemporary Literary Theories*, pp. 3, 6, 7, 9, 11, 12, 14, 16, 23. Troy, N.Y.: Whitston, 1984.

Kuhns, Richard. "Recent Treatments of Tragedy." Review of *The Tragic Vision: Variations on a Theme in Literary Interpretation* (1960). *Journal of Aesthetics and Art Criticism* (Fall 1961), 20(3):93–94.

Landry, Hilton J. Review of *A Window to Criticism: Shakespeare's 'Sonnets' and Modern Poetics* (1964). *Shakespeare Studies* (1965), 1:328–332.

Lane, Lauriat, Jr. Review of *Northrop Frye in Modern Criticism* (1966). *Fiddlehead* (Summer 1967), 72:83, 85–86.

Leitch, Vincent B. *American Literary Criticism from the Thirties to the Eighties*, pp. 25, 33, 34, 39, 45–52, 57, 58, 76, 77, 176, 180, 249, 270, 303, 416nn24, 25. New York: Columbia University Press, 1988.

——Review of *Theory of Criticism: A Tradition and Its System* (1976). *Clio* (Spring 1978), 7(3):463–466.

——"Saving Poetry: Murray Krieger's Faith in Formalism." *New Orleans Review* (Spring 1983), 10(1):12–17. Reprinted in Bruce Henricksen, ed., *Murray Krieger and Contemporary Critical Theory*, pp. 29–41. Irvine Studies in the Humanities. New York: Columbia University Press, 1986.

Lemon, Lee T. *The Partial Critics*, pp. 37, 52, 107, 159–161, 253n35, 254n21, 258n1, 261n4. New York: Oxford University Press, 1965.

——Review of *Northrop Frye in Modern Criticism* (1966). *Prairie Schooner* (Fall 1967), 41(3):356.

Lentricchia, Frank. *After the New Criticism*, pp. xii–xiii, 16, 19, 29–30, 44, 64, 70, 158–159, 163, 169, 171, 184–185, 213–254, 268–269, 294, 336, 349–350. Chicago and London: University of Chicago Press, 1980.

Lerner, Laurence. Review of *A Window to Criticism: Shakespeare's 'Sonnets' and Modern Poetics* (1964). *Modern Language Review* (July 1965), 60(3):430–432.

Levin, Harry. Review of *A Window to Criticism: Shakespeare 'Sonnets' and Modern Poetics* (1964). *Yale Review* (Winter 1965), 54(2):263–264.

Lodge, David. "Current Critical Theory." Review of *Northrop Frye in Modern Criticism* (1966). *Critical Quarterly* (Spring 1967), 9(1):81–84.

Loop, A. Van Der. Review of *The Classic Vision: The Retreat from Extremity in Modern Literature* (1971). *Dutch Quarterly Review of Anglo-American Letters* (1972), 3:130–133.

Louch, Alfred. Review of Paul Hernadi, ed. *What Is Criticism?* (1981). *Philosophy and Literature* (Fall 1982), 6(1–2):192, 193, 194.

Lyons, John D. and Stephen G. Nichols. "Introduction." In John D. Lyons and

Stephen G. Nichols, eds., *Mimesis: From Mirror to Method, Augustine to Descartes*, p. 10. Hanover, N.H. and London: University Press of New England, 1982.

Mackinnon, Lachlan. "In All Directions." Review of Paul Hernadi, ed., *What is Criticism?* (1981). *TLS [Times Literary Supplement]* (February 5, 1982), 4114:144.

McSweeney, Kerry. Review of *The Play and Place of Criticism* (1967). *Queen's Quarterly* (Winter 1968), 75(4):759–760.

Magee, William H. Review of *The Classic Vision: The Retreat from Extremity in Modern Literature* (1971). *Library Journal* (November 15, 1971), 96(20):3760.

Magliola, Robert. Review of Frank Lentricchia's *After the New Criticism. Modern Fiction Studies* (Winter 1981–82), 27(4):761.

Mailloux, Steven. Review of *Directions for Criticism: Structuralism and Its Alternatives* (1977). *Journal of Aesthetics and Art Criticism* (Fall 1978), 37(1):97–100.

Margolis, Joseph. "Farewell Again to the Aesthetic." In Doug Bolling, ed., *Philosophy and Literature*, pp. 157–168. Art and Philosophy, 3. New York: Haven, 1987.

Martin, Taffy. Review of Frank Lentricchia's *After the New Criticism. Journal of Modern Literature* (1980–81), 8(3–4):400.

Martin, Wallace. "Critical Truth as Necessary Error." In Paul Hernadi, ed., *What is Criticism?*, pp. 89–90, 92. Bloomington: Indiana University Press, 1981.

——"The Epoch of Critical Theory." *Comparative Literature* (Fall 1979), 31(4):323–324, 326.

Massk, Victor Ernest. "Critères de la créativité littéraire." *Cahiers Roumains d'Etudes Littéraires* (1984), 3:144–147.

May, James Boyer. Review of *The New Apologists for Poetry* (1956). *Trace* (August 1956), 12:18–22.

Meiners, R. K. "Marginal Men and Centers of Learning: New Critical Rhetoric and Critical Politics." *New Literary History* (Autumn 1986), 18(1):131.

Merrett, Robert James. "Irony and Theology in *Eloisa to Abelard.*" *Wascana Review* (Spring 1983), 18(1):51n1.

Middlebrook, Jonathan, ed. *Matthew Arnold: 'Dover Beach,'* pp. 144–145. Columbus, Ohio: Merrill, 1970.

Miers, Paul. Review of *Theory of Criticism: A Tradition and Its System* (1976). *MLN* (December 1976), 91(6):1634–1638.

Miller, David M. *The Net of Hephaestus: A Study of Modern Criticism and Metaphysical Metaphor*, pp. 16n10, 114–121, 155–157. The Hague & Paris: Mouton, 1971.

Miller, J. Hillis. "The Antitheses of Criticism: Reflections on the Yale Colloquium." In Richard Macksey, ed., *Velocities of Change: Critical Essays from 'MLN,'* p. 138. Baltimore, and London: Johns Hopkins University Press, 1974.

Misra, Sadananda. "A Critique of the Phenomenological Attack Against the New Criticism." *Bharati-Utkal University Journal—Humanities* (July 1979), 9(16):85–96.

——"Murray Krieger and the Survival of the New Criticism." *Indian Journal of English Studies* (N.S.) (1981–82), 21:149–154.

Mitias, Michael H. Review of *Arts on the Level: The Fall of the Elite Object* (1981).

Canadian Philosophical Reviews/Revue Canadienne de Comptes rendus en Philosophie (April 1983), 3(2):70–72.

Mohan, Devinder. "Limits of Contemporary Contextualism and Romantic Poets' Language: Walter Ong, Murray Krieger, and Gaston Bachelard." *Punjab University Research Bulletin (Arts)* (October 1983), 14(2):93–119.

Molesworth, Charles. "What Theory Knows." Review of Frank Lentricchia's *After the New Criticism*. *Salmagundi* (Winter 1982), 55:246, 247, 248, 249.

Montefiore, Alan. Review of *Arts on the Level: The Fall of the Elite Object* (1981). *Notes and Queries (n.s.)* (June 1983), 30(3):273–274.

Morris, Wesley. "The Critic's Responsibility 'To' and 'For.'" *Western Humanities Review* (Summer 1977), 31(3):265–272.

——*Friday's Footprint: Structuralism and the Articulated Text*, pp. 167, 183–184, 195, 199–200, 208, 236nn143, 1, 5, 242n42, 243n65, 244n12, 245nn24, 35. Columbus: Ohio State University Press, 1979.

——"Murray Krieger: A Departure into Diachrony." *New Orleans Review* (Spring 1983), 10(1):24–33. Reprinted in Bruce Henricksen, ed., *Murray Krieger and Contemporary Critical Theory*, pp. 99–118. Irvine Studies in the Humanities. New York: Columbia University Press, 1986.

——*Towards a New Historicism*, pp. 24, 50n, 116–118, 137, 150, 172, 187–209, 211, 215. Princeton: Princeton University Press, 1972.

Muller, Gary R. Review of *Poetic Presence and Illusion: Essays in Critical History and Theory* (1979). *Library Journal* (March 15, 1980), 107(6):725.

——Review of *Theory of Criticism: A Tradition and Its System* (1976). *Library Journal* (May 15, 1976), 101(10):1213.

Murdoch, Dugald. Review of *Northrop Frye in Modern Criticism* (1966). *Studia Neophilologica* (April 1968), 40(1):258–261.

Nahm, Milton C. Review of *The New Apologists for Poetry* (1956). *MLN* (June 1957), 72(6):456–461.

Neill, Edward. "New Waves of Wisdom." Review of Frank Lentricchia's *After the New Criticism*. *Times Educational Supplement* (March 3, 1981), 3376:27.

Norris, Christopher. *Deconstruction: Theory and Practice*, pp. 126, 135, 150–151. London and New York: Methuen, 1982.

——"Openness." Review of Frank Lentricchia's *After the New Criticism*. *Essays in Criticism* (January 1982), 32(1):89–90, 92.

——"Pope Among the Formalists: Textual Politics and *The Rape of the Lock*." In Richard Machin and Christopher Norris, eds., *Post-Structuralist Readings of English Poetry*, pp. 150–159, 161n23. Cambridge: Cambridge University Press, 1987.

O'Hara, Dan. "The Irony of Revisionism in Contemporary Criticism." Review of Frank Lentricchia's *After the New Criticism*. *Contemporary Literature* (Winter 1982), 23(1):111.

Ohmann, Richard. "Teaching and Studying Literature at the End of Ideology." In Louis Kampf and Paul Lauter, eds., *The Politics of Literature: Dissenting Essays on the Teaching of English*, pp. 137, 142, 148, 156n8, 157n27. New York: Pantheon Books, 1972.

Parker, Hershel. *Flawed Texts and Verbal Icons: Literary Authority in American Fiction,* pp. 3, 23–25, 26, 51, 82, 182. Evanston: Northwestern University Press, 1984.

Pavel, Thomas G. "On Convention and Representation in Narratives." In Doug Bolling, ed., *Philosophy and Literature,* pp. 169–188. Art and Philosophy, 3. New York: Haven, 1987.

Pearce, Roy Harvey. "Historicism Once More." *Kenyon Review* (Autumn 1958), 20(4):560–563, 570.

Perrine, Laurence. Review of *The New Apologists for Poetry* (1956). *Southwest Review* (Autumn 1956), 41:393.

Petrescu, Ionna M. "Murray Krieger's 'Contextualism.' " *Cahiers Roumains d'Etudes Littéraires* (1985), 2:128–136.

Poirier, Michel. Review of *A Window to Criticism: Shakespeare's 'Sonnets' and Modern Poetics* (1964). *Etudes Anglaises* (July–September 1966), 19(3):296–297.

Portnoy, Julius. Review of *The New Apologists for Poetry* (1956). *Journal of Aesthetics and Art Criticism* (June 1958), 16(4):536–537.

Pritchard, J. P. Review of *The New Apologists for Poetry* (1956). *Books Abroad* (Autumn 1956), 30(4):444.

Raaberg, Gwen. *"Ekphrasis* and the Temporal/Spatial Metaphor in Murray Krieger's Critical Theory." *New Orleans Review* (Winter 1985), 12(4):34–43.

Rapaport, Herman. "The Phenomenology of Spenserian Ekphrasis." In Bruce Henricksen, ed., *Murray Krieger and Contemporary Critical Theory,* pp. 157–175. Irvine Studies in the Humanities. New York: Columbia University Press, 1986.

Raval, Suresh. "Contextualism and Poetic Autonomy: Anatomy of a Critical Theory." *Arizona Quarterly* (Winter 1980), 36(4):293–314.

Regan, Mariann Sanders. *Love Words: The Self and the Text in Medieval and Renaissance Poetry,* pp. 39–40, 47–48. 226, 277*n*2, 278*n*18. Ithaca: Cornell University Press, 1982.

Review of *Arts on the Level: The Fall of the Elite Object* (1981). *Choice* (December 1981), 19(4):495.

Review of Bruce Henricksen, ed., *Murray Krieger and Contemporary Critical Theory (1986). American Literature* (October 1986), 58(3):488.

Review of *The Classic Vision: The Retreat from Extremity in Modern Literature* (1971). *American Literature* (November 1972), 44(3):532–533.

Review of *The Classic Vision: The Retreat from Extremity in Modern Literature* (1971). *Choice* (May 1972), 9(3):364.

Review of *The Classic Vision: The Retreat from Extremity in Modern Literature* (1971). *Journal of Modern Literature* (February 1974), 3(3)473.

Review of *The Classic Vision: The Retreat from Extremity in Modern Literature* (1971). *Zigo-Szinzn* (Japan) (September 1972).

Review of *Directions for Criticism: Structuralism and Its Alternatives* (1977). *Choice* (May 1978), 15(3):390.

Review of *The New Apologists for Poetry* (1956). *The Globe* (Sioux City, Iowa) (May 17, 1956).

Review of *The New Apologists for Poetry* (1956). *Journal* (Wilmington, Delaware) (January 1958):15.

Review of *The New Apologists for Poetry* (1956). *Kirkus Reviews* (March 1, 1956), 24:205.

Review of *The New Apologists for Poetry* (1956). *News Leader* (Richmond, Virginia) (August 6, 1956).

Review of *The New Apologists for Poetry* (1956). *Regesten* (Spring 1957):52–53.

Review of *Northrop Frye in Modern Criticism* (1966). *Hibernia* (Dublin) (February 1967).

Review of *Northrop Frye in Modern Criticism* (1966). *Yale Review* (Spring 1967), 56(3):vi, xii.

Review of *The Play and Place of Criticism* (1967). *Choice* (September 1968), 5(7): 778.

Review of *The Play and Place of Criticism* (1967). *Uitzending O Dinslag* (October 1969).

Review of *The Play and Place of Criticism* (1967). *Virginia Quarterly Review* (Autumn 1967), 43(4):clxiv.

Review of *Poetic Presence and Illusion: Essays in Critical History and Theory* (1979). *Choice* (July–August 1980), 17(5–6):666.

Review of *Poetic Presence and Illusion: Essays in Critical History and Theory* (1979). *Virginia Quarterly Review* (Summer 1980), 56(3):92.

Review of *Theory of Criticism: A Tradition and Its System* (1976). *Choice* (November 1976), 13(9):1130.

Review of *Theory of Criticism: A Tradition and Its System* (1976). *Virginia Quarterly Review* (Winter 1978), 54(1):13–14.

Review of *The Tragic Vision: Variations on a Theme in Literary Interpretation* (1960). *Modern Fiction Studies* (Winter 1960–61), 6(4):376.

Review of *The Tragic Vision: Variations on a Theme in Literary Interpretation* (1960). *New York Herald Tribune Book Review* (February 19, 1961):37.

Review of *The Tragic Vision: Variations on a Theme in Literary Interpretation* (1960). *Nineteenth-Century Fiction* (December 1960), 15(3):280.

Review of *The Tragic Vision: Variations on a Theme in Literary Interpretation* (1960). *Wisconsin Library Bulletin* (March 1961), 57:116.

Review of *A Window to Criticism: Shakespeare's 'Sonnets' and Modern Poetics* (1964). *Choice* (September 1964), 1(7):241–242.

Review of *A Window to Criticism: Shakespeare's 'Sonnets' and Modern Poetics* (1964). *Des Moines Register* (April 1964).

Review of *A Window to Criticism: Shakespeare's 'Sonnets' and Modern Poetics* (1964). *San Francisco Examiner* (April 1964).

Review of *A Window to Criticism: Shakespeare's 'Sonnets' and Modern Poetics* (1964). *Scholarly Books in America* (July 1964), 6(1):40.

Review of *A Window to Criticism: Shakespeare's 'Sonnets' and Modern Poetics* (1964). *Washington Post* (April 1964).

Rewa, Michael P., Jr., Review of *The New Apologists for Poetry* (1956). *Emerson Society Quarterly* (1958), 12:53–54.

Riddel, Joseph N. "Scriptive Fate/Scriptive Hope." Review of Edward W. Said's *Beginnings*. *Diacritics* (Fall 1976), 6(3):23n1.

Robie, Burton A. Review of *A Window to Criticism: Shakespeare's 'Sonnets' and Modern Poetics* (1964). *Library Journal* (May 15, 1964), 89:2097.

Rodway, Allan. Review of *The Classic Vision: The Retreat from Extremity in Modern Literature* (1971). *Notes and Queries* (N.S.) (September 1975), 22(9):429–431.

——Review of *Northrop Frye in Modern Criticism* (1966). *Notes and Queries* (N.S.) (July 1967), 14(7):272–274.

Rose, Mark, "Criticism as Quest: Murray Krieger and the Pursuit of Presence." *New Orleans Review* (Spring 1983), 10(1):8–11. Reprinted in Bruce Henricksen, ed., *Murray Krieger and Contemporary Critical Theory,* pp. 21–28. Irvine Studies in the Humanities. New York: Columbia University Press, 1986.

Rosenthal, M. L. Review of *The Play and Place of Criticism* (1967). *Poetry* (May 1969), 114(2):130–132.

Rosmarin, Adena. "Rereading Contextualism." In Bruce Henricksen, ed., *Murray Krieger and Contemporary Critical Theory,* pp. 56–77. Irvine Studies in the Humanities. New York: Columbia University Press, 1986.

Ross, Steven David. "The Inexhaustibility of the Medium." In Doug Bolling, ed., *Philosophy and Literature,* pp. 53–67. Art and Philosophy, 3. New York: Haven, 1987.

Rowe, John Carlos. "James's Rhetoric of the Eye: Re-marking the Impression." *Criticism* (Summer 1982), 24(3):239, 246–247, 250–252.

Rudin, Seymour. "Tragic Vision in the Modern Novel." Review of *The Tragic Vision: Variations on a Theme in Literary Interpretation* (1960). *Massachusetts Review* (Autumn 1960), 2(1):174–177.

Sage, Lorna. "The Fiction of the Critic." Review of *Theory of Criticism: A Tradition and Its System* (1976). *New Review* (London) (January–February 1977), 3(34–35):68–69.

Said, Edward W. "Roads Taken and Not Taken in Contemporary Criticism." *Contemporary Literature* (Summer 1976), 17(3):327n1.

Salinger, Herman. Review of *The Tragic Vision: Variations on a Theme in Literary Interpretation* (1960). *South Atlantic Quarterly* (Summer 1961), 60(3):372.

Sandeen, Ernest. "Recent Criticism." Review of *The Play and Place of Criticism* (1967). *Poetry* (August 1968), 112(5):358–359.

Schleifer, Ronald. "Enunciation and Genre: Mikhail Bakhtin and the 'Double-voiced Narration' of *The Rape of the Lock.*" *New Orleans Review* (Winter 1988), 15(4):39.

Schlueter, Paul. "Born of Crisis and Shock." Review of *The Tragic Vision: Variations on a Theme in Literary Interpretation* (1960). *Christian Century* (August 23, 1961), 78(34):1007.

Schneider, Franz. Review of *The Tragic Vision: Variations on a Theme in Literary Interpretation* (1960). *Thought* (Autumn 1961), 36(142):458–459.

Scholes, Robert. Review of *Theory of Criticism: A Tradition and Its System* (1976). *New Republic* (October 23, 1976), 175(17):27–28.

Schwab, Gabrielle. "Reader-Response and the Aesthetic Experience of Otherness." *Stanford Literature Review* (Spring 1986), 3(1):132–133.

Schwartz, Elias. Review of *The Tragic Vision: Variations on a Theme in Literary Interpretation* (1960). *College English* (January 1961), 22(4):288.

Servotte, H. Review of *A Window to Criticism: Shakespeare's 'Sonnets' and Modern Poetics* (1964). *Leuvense Bijdragen* (Supplement: *Bijblad*) (1965), 54(2): 64–66.

Sewall, Richard B. Review of *The Tragic Vision: Variations on a Theme in Literary Interpretation* (1960). *Yale Review* (Summer 1961), 50(3):436–437.

——*The Vision of Tragedy,* pp. 150–151. New Haven: Yale University Press, 1959. New, enlarged edition, pp. 177–178, 198n108. New Haven:Yale University Press, 1980.

Shiner, Larry. Review of *Arts on the Level: The Fall of the Elite Object* (1981). *Philosophy and Literature* (Fall 1982), 61(1–2):221–222.

Shusterman, Richard. *T. S. Eliot and the Philosophy of Criticism,* pp. 130–132. New York: Columbia University Press, 1988.

Sircello, Guy. "The Poetry of Theory: Reflections on *After the New Criticism.*" *Journal of Aesthetics and Art Criticism* (Summer 1984), 42(4):388–396.

Skulsky, Harold. "Reflections on Murray Krieger's Defense of Poetics." In Doug Bolling, ed., *Philosophy and Literature,* pp. 117–128. Art and Philosophy, 3. New York: Haven, 1987.

Smith, Barbara Herrnstein. *Contingencies of Value: Alternative Perspectives for Critical Theory,* pp. 188n1, 197n18. Cambridge: Harvard University Press, 1988.

Smith, T. Francis. Review of *The New Apologists for Poetry* (1956). *Library Journal* (May 1, 1956), 81(9):1179.

Spears, Monroe K. Review of *The Classic Vision: The Retreat from Extremity in Modern Literature* (1971). *English Language Notes* (June 1973), 10(4):310–313.

Spector, Robert D. Review of *Poetic Presence and Illusion: Essays in Critical History and Theory* (1979). *World Literature Today* (Summer 1980), 54(3):494.

Stade, George. "*Parole* into *Ecriture:* A Response to Murray Krieger." *Boundary 2* (1979), 8(1):123–127. Reprinted in William V. Spanos, Paul A. Bove and Daniel O'Hara, eds., *The Question of Textuality: Strategies of Reading in Contemporary American Criticism,* pp. 123–127. Bloomington: Indiana University Press, 1982.

    A response to Krieger's "Poetic Presence and Illusion II: Formalist Theory and the Duplicity of Metaphor" (1979), (1982).

Steinmetz, Lee, ed. *Analyzing Literary Works: A Guide for College Students,* pp. 112–113. Evanston, Ill: Row, Peterson, 1962.

Stolnitz, Jerome. Review of *Arts on the Level: The Fall of the Elite Object* (1981). *Journal of Aesthetic Education* (Winter 1982), 16(4):99–102.

Strelka, Joseph P. *Methodologie der Literaturwissenschaft,* pp. 59, 68, 194, 300, 355, 357, 380, 396. Tubingen: Niemeyer, 1978.

Strozier, Robert M. Review of *Theory of Criticism: A Tradition and Its System* (1976). *Criticism* (Summer 1977), 19(3):275–278.

Subbarao, C. "Contextualist Poetics and the Nature of Language." *Literary Criterion* (Bombay) (Winter 1969), 9(1):54–60.

Surdulescu, Radu. "De sine a fictiunii poetica prezentei sau constiinta." ["The Poetics of Presence and the Self-Consciousness of Fiction."] In Murray Krieger, *Teoria criticii: Traditie si sistem,* pp. 5–17. Bucharest: Univers, 1982.
    Introduction to the Romanian translation (by Radu Surdulescu) of *Theory of Criticism: A Tradition and Its System* (1976).

Sutherland, John. "Ivory Institutes." *TLS [Times Literary Supplement]* (December 18–24, 1987), 4420:1402.

Sutton, Walter. "The Contextualist Dilemma—Or Fallacy?" *Journal of Aesthetics and Art Criticism* (December 1958), 17(2):219–229.

——"Contextualist Theory and Criticism as a Social Act." *Journal of Aesthetics and Art Criticism* (1960–61), 19:317–325.

——"Letters Pro and Con." *Journal of Aesthetics and Art Criticism* (Spring 1963), 21(3):347.

——*Modern American Criticism,* pp. 219, 265. Englewood Cliffs, N.J.: Prentice-Hall, 1963.

Swiggart, Peter. Review of *The Tragic Vision: Variations on a Theme in Literary Interpretation* (1960). *Criticism* (Winter 1962), 4(1):82–84.

Tibbs, Molly. "American Literary Theory." Review of Frank Lentricchia's *After the New Criticism. Contemporary Review* (May 1984), 244(1420):275.

Unterecker, John. Review of *The Tragic Vision: Variations on a Theme in Literary Interpretation* (1960). *Champaign-Urbana (Ill.) Courier* (October 2, 1960).

Vivas, Eliseo. "Contextualism Reconsidered." *Journal of Aesthetics and Art Criticism* (December 1959), 18(2):222–240.

Von Hendy, André. Review of *Northrop Frye in Modern Criticism* (1966). *Criticism* (Fall 1967), 9(4):393–395.

W., G. F. Review of *Poetic Presence and Illusion: Essays in Critical History and Theory* (1979). *Sydney Newsletter* (1981), 2(1):12–13.

Watkins, Evan. *The Critical Act: Criticism and Community,* pp. 6–7, 19–20, 25–26, 60. New Haven and London: Yale University Press, 1978.

——"The Self-Evaluations of Critical Theory." *Boundary 2* (Spring-Fall 1984), 12(3),13(1):359–378.

Watson, George. *The Literary Critics: A Study of English Descriptive Criticism,* 2d ed., p. 230. London: Woburn Press, 1973; p. 232. London: Hogarth Press, 1986.

Watt, Ian. *Conrad in the Nineteenth Century,* p. 237n14. Berkeley and Los Angeles: University of California Press, 1979.

Watts, Harold M. Review of *Theory of Criticism: A Tradition and Its System* (1976). *Modern Fiction Studies* (Summer 1977), 23(2):307–310.

Webster, Grant. *The Republic of Letters: A History of Postwar American Literary Opinion,* pp. 24–25, 34–35, 37, 42, 64, 82, 118–119, 176–177, 190–202, 315n66, 325n3, 328n41, 354–355. Baltimore and London: Johns Hopkins University Press, 1979.

——Review of *Poetic Presence and Illusion: Essays in Critical History and Theory* (1979), *Style* (Fall 1981), 15(4):495–496.

Weinsheimer, Joel. "On Going Home Again: New Criticism Revisited." Review of *Theory of Criticism: A Tradition and Its System* (1976) *PTL* (1977), 2(3): 563–577.

Wellek, René. "American Criticism of the Last Ten Years." In Alfred Weber and Dietmar Haack, eds., *Amerikanische Literatur im 20. Jahrhundert: American Literature in the 20th Century*, pp. 19–20. Reprinted in René Wellek, *The Attack on Literature and Other Essays*, pp. 110–111. Chapel Hill, N.C.: University of North Carolina Press, 1982.

——"An End to Criticism?" Review of Grant Webster's *The Republic of Letters: A History of Postwar American Literary Opinion. Georgia Review* (Spring 1980), 34(1):183.

——"The History of Dostoevsky Criticism." In René Wellek, *Discriminations: Further Concepts of Criticism*, p. 325. New Haven and London: Yale University Press, 1970.

——*A History of Modern Criticism: 1750–1950, Vol. 6: American Criticism, 1900–1950*, p. 150. New Haven: Yale University Press, 1986.

——"Literary Criticism." In Wolfgang Fleischmann, ed., *Encyclopedia of World Literature in the 20th Century*, 2:325. New York: Ungar, 1969.

——"The New Criticism: Pro and Contra." *Critical Inquiry* (Summer 1978), 4(4): 617–618.

——"The 19th-Century Russian Novel in English and American Criticism." In John Garrard, ed., *The Russian Novel from Pushkin to Pasternak*, pp. 267–268. New Haven and London: Yale University Press, 1983.

——"Philosophy and Postwar American Criticism." In René Wellek, *Concepts of Criticism*, p. 341. New Haven and London: Yale University Press, 1963.

——Review of *The New Apologists for Poetry* (1956). *Yale Review* (Autumn 1956), 46(1):114–116.

West, Robert H. Review of *The Tragic Vision: Variations on a Theme in Literary Interpretation* (1960). *Georgia Review* (Spring 1962), 16(1):102–104.

White, Hayden. "The Absurdist Moment in Contemporary Literary Theory." *Contemporary Literature* (Summer 1976), 17(3):378n1.

Wicht, Wolfgang. Review of *Theory of Criticism: A Tradition and Its System* (1976). *Referatedienst zur Literaturwissenschaft* (1982), 14:15–16.

Wieck, David Thoreau. Review of *The Play and Place of Criticism* (1967). *Journal of Aesthetics and Art Criticism* (Winter 1969), 28(2):250–251.

Wimsatt, William K., Jr. *Day of the Leopards*, pp. xii, 183, 188–195, 203. New Haven and London: Yale University Press, 1976.

——*Hateful Contraries: Studies in Literature and Criticism*, pp. 24–25, 43–44, 243. Lexington: University of Kentucky Press, 1965.

——"Responsio Scribleri." *CEA Chap Book* [Supplement to *CEA Critic*] (December 1963), 26(3):34–35.

——Review of *The Tragic Vision: Variations on a Theme in Literary Interpretation* (1960). *JEGP* (January 1962), 61(1):140–144.

——Review of *A Window to Criticism: Shakespeare's 'Sonnets' and Modern Poetics* (1964). *Modern Philology* (August 1966), 64(1):71–74.

Wimsatt, William K., Jr. and Cleanth Brooks. *Literary Criticism: A Short History. Vol. 2: Romantic and Modern Criticism,* pp. 678–679. Chicago and London: University of Chicago Press, 1978.

Yeghiayan, Eddie. "A Checklist of Writings By and About Murray Krieger." *New Orleans Review* (Spring 1983), 10(1):63–78.

Young. Robert, "Literary Theory." *The Year's Work in English Studies* (1981), 62: 18, 43.

——"Literary Theory." *The Year's Work in English Studies* (1982), 63:492, 500, 501.

INDEX